BRUSHY BILL

BRUSHY BILL

PROOF THAT HIS CLAIM TO BE BILLY THE KID WAS A HOAX

ROY L. HAWS

SUNSTONE
PRESS

SANTA FE

Sunstone books may be purchased for educational, business, or sales promotional use.
For information please write: Special Markets Department, Sunstone Press,
P.O. Box 2321, Santa Fe, New Mexico 87504-2321.

Book and cover design › Vicki Ahl
Body typeface › Trebuchet MS
Printed on acid-free paper
∞
eBook 978-1-61139-368-2

Library of Congress Cataloging-in-Publication Data

Haws, Roy L.
  Brushy Bill : proof that his claim to be Billy the Kid was a hoax / by Roy L. Haws.
    pages cm
Includes bibliographical references and index.
  ISBN 978-1-63293-055-2 (softcover : alk. paper)
  1. Billy, the Kid--Death and burial. 2. Roberts, Oliver Pleasant, 1879-1950. 3. Impostors
and imposture--United States--Case studies. 4. Outlaws Biography.--Southwest, New 5.
Southwest, New--Biography. I. Title.
  F786.B54H39 2015
  364.16'33092--dc23
  [B]
                            2015004144

WWW.SUNSTONEPRESS.COM
SUNSTONE PRESS / POST OFFICE BOX 2321 / SANTA FE, NM 87504-2321 /USA
(505) 988-4418 / ORDERS ONLY (800) 243-5644 / FAX (505) 988-1025

"Brushy Bill" Roberts. Photograph courtesy of Stacy Canion.

Brushy Bill (Oliver Pleasant Roberts). Pencil Sketch by Linda Weatherman.

DEDICATION

This book is dedicated to
my wonderful wife
Barbara Jean Martin Haws
*(for putting up with me during the
entire process of this writing
experience).*

CONTENTS

ACKNOWLEDGEMENTS

A number of my friends and family members aided me during the editing of my book. I would first like to acknowledge and thank our family friend, Diedra Germany Clark, for her tireless efforts in helping remove some of the confusion from my rather complicated narrative. Although my original text made perfect sense to me, Diedra greatly helped in our joint effort of modifying sentence and paragraph constructions for improved reader clarity. I will always be grateful for her thoughtful aid in my first and likely only writing endeavor.

I would like to acknowledge others that have read portions of my text and provided constructive comments and suggestions. In no particular order, these individuals are: Kristina Glenn, Richard Freeze, Phil Waller, Barbara Jean Martin Haws (my wife), and my wonderful mother-in-law, Dorothy Martin. Additional thanks go to my wife, Barbara, for key genealogical research and gravesite pictures.

Great thanks go to my wonderful neighbor, friend, and talented artist, Linda Weatherman. She provided marvelous pencil sketches used throughout this book. Linda would not even accept payment for her incredible artwork.

Special thanks are in order for my Uncle Paul Emerson for his conversations and correspondence with me during my writing process. He provided a needed family photo of the Henry Oliver Roberts family which included an image of Brushy (Oliver Pleasant Roberts), while still a teenager. Also included in my book is a 1986 letter he penned to Mr. William A. Tunstill providing additional insight in regard to Brushy's true identity as Oliver Pleasant Roberts. Thank you Uncle Paul.

My final "thank you" goes to all my friends and family members for their support and encouragement during my extensive six-month research, writing, and editing endeavor.

Brushy Bill Roberts with William V. Morrison. Pencil Sketch by Linda Weatherman.

Introduction

For well over a century, one of the more fascinating Wild West episodes capturing the imagination of historians, writers, and public is the legend of Billy the Kid. This colorful, historical figure has often been visited in books, newspapers, magazines, movies, and documentary films.

Many unanswered questions have contributed to the mystery surrounding the legendary outlaw. One basic question often asked is: "Did Pat Garrett really kill Billy the Kid on the night of July 14, 1881?" Over the years many books and articles, historical and fictional, have addressed that question. None have produced compelling evidence one way or the other to completely satisfy everyone. Conflicting accounts of events have led many to believe Billy the Kid was not killed that night in 1881. It may never be known to everyone's satisfaction whether or not Pat killed Billy. My book will not address or attempt to answer that question. It will, however, concentrate solely on the myth that one certain individual was the historical Billy the Kid, living on to a ripe old age.

Many believe the leading claim of Billy the Kid surviving past that July night in 1881 belongs to a flamboyant individual calling himself Brushy Bill Roberts. Brushy contended he was, in fact, Billy the Kid. If his story was true, then Billy the Kid lived a long life of nearly 91 years. However, with all contentions and presumptions aside, what we do know is a man identified as Brushy Bill Roberts died from a massive heart attack on the streets of Hico, Texas December 27, 1950.

Just what would lead me to indulge in yet another effort affirming or disclaiming a facet of this Wild West episode? The answer is: I have a direct genealogical connection with a storytelling relative who crafted a myth that intertwined with my family's lore. Brushy's incredible farce achieved national popularity following the publication of *Alias Billy the Kid*. (Sonnichsen, Morrison, 1955)

In this book, I'll unravel who Brushy Bill Roberts really was and disprove his alleged identity as Billy the Kid. After considerable research and a substantial review of works of others, I've confidently concluded that Brushy Bill Roberts was actually Oliver Pleasant Roberts, born August 26, 1879 and did die on the streets of Hico, Texas from a massive heart attack December 27, 1950 at the age of 71. Brushy was, in fact, my maternal half great-granduncle and was just under two years of age the night Pat Garrett is said to have killed Billy the Kid.

Having studied a number of books regarding the Brushy Bill persona, I wish to acknowledge the works of a few authors.

The first work, titled *Alias Billy the Kid*, was published in 1955 and written by C. L. Sonnichsen and William V. Morrison. This narrative primarily consists of transcribed recorded interviews that began in June 1949 between William V. Morrison and Brushy Bill Roberts. This book is considered the authority for Brushy's statements, yet over the years has become the source of considerable controversy.

Certain researchers and authors believe Brushy was coached during the taped interviews. They believe Mr. Morrison prompted Brushy with information allowing for a more believable story. There is no way to know if this occurred or not; the recordings are not available to examine. I have accepted the transcriptions as accurate recordings of Brushy's statements and have not attempted to claim otherwise.

The second work I acknowledge is an excellent book titled *Billy the Kid, His Real Name Was...* by Jim Johnson, published in 2006. Mr. Johnson raised many issues with Brushy's story and aided my analysis with his genealogical research.

The third work I acknowledge is titled *Billy the Kid's Pretenders* by Gale Cooper, published in 2010. In her book, Ms. Cooper examined two pretenders, Brushy Bill Roberts and John Miller. The author identified areas of conflict within Brushy's confabulations I might have otherwise overlooked. Although I differ in opinion with Ms. Cooper regarding her implications of Mr. Morrison prompting Brushy with historical information, her book certainly provided helpful insights.

Many "Brushy believers" exist, who even when presented with a preponderance of genealogical evidence and conflicts within Brushy's tale, will continue to believe he was Billy the Kid. If you are one of these believers, I propose you read no further; you should simply discard this book. If, however, you are willing to evaluate what I believe to be an accurate and logical discussion, then please read on.

This book should convince most that Brushy Bill Roberts was not Billy the Kid. It should become clear Brushy was a colorful individual with the daydream of becoming someone important. It is my contention that at some time after the mid-1930s, he initiated construction of a fantastic myth aimed at fulfilling his psychological needs of notoriety. Subsequent to his death in 1950, his stated narrative was further enhanced by clever authors with creative genealogy, modifications of historical events, and time conflict solutions in their attempt to provide undeserved credibility to Brushy's tall tale.

Since publication of *Alias Billy the Kid* (again, Sonnichsen, Morrison, 1955), many books, articles, and television programs have featured the Brushy Bill Roberts' faux-history. Other authors, intent on debunking the Brushy saga, generally spotlighted time conflicts and historical errors. In my analysis, I will identify genealogical fabrications by Brushy and "believer" book authors. The genealogical evidence alone proves Brushy was not Billy the Kid. However, my subsequent analysis of timeline conflicts, historical errors, and testimonials should convince even the most diehard believers that Brushy was not Billy.

Conscientious reading of this book is recommended. I propose the reader digest the information and discussion slowly, as particular sections become necessarily complicated due to numerous date, name, and genealogical discussions. These areas may be difficult to follow without continual thought.

Brushy's Original Headstone in Hamilton, Texas.

Brushy's Current Headstone in Hamilton, Texas. Note the change in name and the year of birth from 1868 to 1859 to fit with Brushy's fable.

(Actual birth year of Oliver Pleasant Roberts was 1879.)

The Story Begins. William V. Morrison Interviews with Brushy

In June 1949, an elderly man, know as Brushy Bill Roberts, met with probate investigator William V. Morrison. Brushy purported the fantastic claim he was, in fact, the true Billy the Kid. Over the course of a year, Mr. Morrison completed a series of taped interviews with Brushy. These interviews were published in 1955 in a book written by C. L. Sonnichsen and William V. Morrison titled *Alias Billy the Kid*.

Controversy began immediately after publication and continues to date. Many individuals believe Brushy's tall tale to be true, while others do not. A number of books have been published accepting Brushy's cock-and-bull yarn. My narrative provides substantial evidence and discussion resulting in the only logical conclusion, Brushy Bill Roberts was not Billy the Kid.

In the Morrison interviews, Brushy voiced a number of assertions. He declared his birth name as William Henry Roberts and proceeded by describing his life and events before, during, and after the Lincoln County War in New Mexico. Brushy professed to be the historical Billy the Kid using aliases of William H. Bonney, Henry McCarty, Henry Antrim, and others during his years in New Mexico. Furthermore, Brushy contended a companion known as Billy Barlow was the actual person killed by Pat Garrett the night of July 14, 1881.

Is it possible Pat Garrett killed the wrong man that night? By some accounts, the only witnesses observing the body were Sheriff Pat Garrett and his deputies, Thomas (Kip) McKinney and John Poe. From their own accounts, neither McKinney nor Poe had ever before met Billy the Kid. After the killing, some have insisted Billy was immediately covered with a sheet, guarded the remainder of the night, and hastily buried in Fort Sumner, New Mexico the following morning. Others, however, have insisted Billy's body was viewed by many after his supposed death. In addition, Pat Garrett never collected the governor's promised $500 reward. Over the years, many issues with Pat Garrett's account of events have contributed to substantial controversy.

Many believe Billy the Kid escaped death that July night in 1881. Perhaps he did, I don't know. Many writings from respected historians exist on this topic. I, however, will concentrate on the false claim of a deceased elderly man, known as Brushy Bill Roberts, that he was, in fact, the real Billy the Kid.

Pat Garrett (1850–1908) from the Rose Collection, Image 1782, Western History Collections, University of Oklahoma Libraries.

Name and Date Problems Begin

Although Brushy professed using multiple monikers through a significant portion of his life, all recorded public documents reflect his identity as a variation of the name Oliver Pleasant Roberts. Census, marriage, and other documents clearly show Brushy's use of the names Ollie Roberts, Ollie P. Roberts, Oliver P. Roberts, and O. P. Roberts. During the final years of his life, Brushy began using the middle initial *L* instead of *P*. Documents from his fourth marriage to Malinda Allison in 1945 show his name as O. L. Roberts, although no one seems to know what the middle initial *L* was intended to abbreviate. Pertinent documents illustrating Brushy's lifelong use of derivations of the name Oliver Pleasant Roberts are included in the appendices of this book.

If Brushy was not Oliver Pleasant Roberts, why would he use a form of the name Oliver on all documents throughout his life? While allegedly employed with the U.S. Marshall Service, Brushy avouched discovering the body of his cousin, Ollie Roberts, who was mistakenly killed in a horse theft incident. Brushy reported collecting dead Ollie's belongings with the intent of returning them to the Roberts family in Sulphur Springs, Texas. To his great surprise, Brushy insisted Ollie's mother embraced him and took him to her bosom. She then mistakenly declared him as her long lost son returning home after running away in about 1884. Brushy maintained it was at this point he assumed the identity of his dead cousin, Ollie Roberts. During his alleged visit to the Roberts family residence, Brushy refers to Martha as his cousin and wife of Dudley Heath. Although no specific year is given for this portion of Brushy's whopper, based on the progression of his narrative it appears to have been in 1892.

For clarity, I feel it now pertinent to relate actual genealogical connections. Martha Vada Roberts Heath (my great-grandmother) was the daughter of Henry Oliver Roberts from his first marriage to Caroline Dunn.

Martha Vada was married to Monroe Dudley Heath. Henry Oliver Roberts' second marriage was to Sara Elizabeth Ferguson. The third child from this marriage was Oliver Pleasant Roberts born August 26, 1879.

Henry Oliver Roberts (about 1920), father of Brushy (Oliver Pleasant Roberts) from the author's family collection.

Brushy referred to cousin Ollie's family in Sulphur Springs, Texas including Martha and her husband, Dudley Heath. My maternal ancestral family includes Martha Vada, Dudley Heath, and Oliver Pleasant Roberts, meeting all criteria stated by Brushy in his narrative. During this period of time, my Roberts family resided in Sulphur Springs, Texas. It is clear Brushy was referring to my Roberts family.

In the Morrison interviews, Brushy asserted his actual date of birth as December 31, 1859. With this date of birth, Brushy would be age appropriate for Billy the Kid when Pat Garrett is alleged to have killed him in 1881.

With Brushy's stated year of birth of 1859, the age difference between Brushy and Oliver Pleasant Roberts, born in 1879, would be about 20 years. With this extreme age difference, the truth of Brushy's acceptance by Ollie's mother in 1892 as her long lost son would appear suspect. This strange and unlikely scenario would require Sara Elizabeth Ferguson Roberts and Henry Oliver Roberts accepting a 33 year old Brushy as their long lost 13 year old son. Would this appear reasonable?

The narrative proclaimed by Brushy would necessitate one to believe a 33 year man not only passed himself off as a 13 year old teenager, yet successfully assumed his identity on public documents throughout his life. If this isn't difficult enough to accept, Brushy's statement of Ollie running away from home in 1884 is suspect as well. This absurd storyline would necessitate a very young Ollie fleeing the security of his parents' home at the tender age of five. I believe this to be a nonsensical stretch of imagination, don't you?

A small collection of Brushy believers in their attempt to rationalize and solve the age difficulty, assert an older brother also named Oliver or Ollie existed. I have a full listing of Oliver's siblings (included in the appendices), but let's examine the silly assertion an older unrecorded sibling also named Oliver existed. Sara Elizabeth and Henry Oliver married May 14, 1876. It would be chronologically impossible for a brother, also named Ollie, to be more than a couple of years older than Oliver Pleasant Roberts born in 1879. Of additional importance, records reflect Oliver Pleasant Roberts as the third child of Henry Oliver Roberts and his wife, Sara Elizabeth. Even with this strange scenario of two sons named Oliver, the older with no public records, the age difficulty remains. Regardless of the unlikely existence of an older Oliver, an over 30 year old would still be passing himself off as a teenager. In addition, if Brushy had assumed the identity of an older Oliver, why would he have used the name of the younger, Oliver Pleasant throughout his life?

An additional Brushy believer has derived an even more fantastic rationalization of a two Oliver theory. This theory entails a highly unlikely scenario raising even more questions than are answered. In view of the unrealistic and complicated nature of this storyline, I have included a chapter titled "The Theory of Two Olivers" in the latter portion of my book. Hopefully, by the time you reach this chapter, you should already be adequately convinced Brushy was not Billy the Kid. In this case, you may simply disregard that chapter and move directly to my final chapter titled "In Conclusion."

Brushy stated in one portion of a Morrison interview never referring to himself by his avowed birth name of William Henry Roberts beyond the age of three. However, during a later interview with Morrison, Brushy denied using this name beyond his early teens. It is true no public records or documents show Brushy as William Henry Roberts. Documentation is substantial Brushy only used the names Oliver Pleasant Roberts, Oliver Roberts, Ollie Roberts, Ollie P. Roberts, O. P. Roberts, O. L. Roberts, Oliver L. Roberts, and Ollie L. Roberts throughout his life. I note the middle initial *L* was never used in any public documents located prior to his marriage to Malinda Allison in 1945. However, during the interviews with Morrison, Brushy reported using the name O. L. Roberts or Oliver L. Roberts during most of his life, revealing yet another considerable inconsistency in his myth. I have a logical theory why Brushy abandoned the middle initial *P* in favor of *L*, as well as a change in his birth year. I discuss details of these changes in a later chapter.

Brushy used the above derivations of Oliver in all census records, draft registration, marriages, divorce documents, purchase of real estate, and sale of real estate. Marriage records show Brushy married four times, mentioning all in his Morrison interviews with the exception of his first wife Anna Lee. Using the name of O. P. Roberts, he married Anna Lee, July 11, 1909, later divorcing her November 10, 1910. Based on divorce documents, his first marriage was a troubled one, lasting little more than a year. Perhaps this Texas marriage and divorce represented some unpleasant memories Brushy believed unworthy of mentioning. However, during these same years, the dates of Brushy's marriage conflict with his reported timeline of living in Mexico. I will later discuss this time conflict among many others.

The Magical Aging of Ollie/Brushy

In the recorded interviews with William V. Morrison, Brushy proclaimed assuming the identity of his deceased cousin, Ollie, around 1892. Census records between 1880 and 1930 reflect appropriate ages for Oliver Pleasant Roberts born in 1879. However, a drastic increase of Ollie's age began with the 1940 census. Upon his death, Brushy's widow reported 1868 as his year of birth. His original tombstone included 1868 as his birth year, along with his name as Ollie L. Roberts.

On the 1880 census, Oliver Roberts is shown as one year old (his name was spelled Olover). On the 1900 census, well after Brushy alleged to have assumed the identity of Ollie in 1892, Oliver Pleasant Roberts is shown as age 21, still living with his parents. On the 1910 census, Oliver P. Roberts, aka Brushy, is shown as 30 years of age. The 1920 census records Oliver P. Roberts as age 41. On the 1930 census, Brushy's name shows as Oliver Roberts, 52 years of age (still consistent with someone born in 1879). Mysteriously, the 1940 census, a mere ten years later, shows Brushy's name Ollie, age 70. He surprisingly aged 18 years between the 1930 and 1940 censuses. Ollie (Brushy) is now age appropriate of someone born at the end of 1868. The birth year of 1868 is subsequently used by Brushy on public documents and is also the year placed on his original tombstone by his widow, Malinda.

Why the change in birth year from 1879 to 1868 and when did this change happen? I believe the change occurred between 1936 and 1940. I am also convinced Brushy began using the middle initial L instead of P during this same time. President Franklin D. Roosevelt signed into law the Social Security Bill on August 14, 1935. Old-age assistance was provided for needy persons age 65 or older. The federal share was a maximum of $15 per month matched by the state. Texas began enrolling and providing income for those over the age of 65 in 1936. Oliver Pleasant Roberts, with a birth year of 1879, would have been only 57 years of age in 1936. I propose Brushy, a Texas resident, altered his birth year from 1879 to 1868, falsely qualifying for benefits. The alteration of his middle initial would help camouflage the potential discovery of his actual age from public records. With the middle initial change to *L* and a birth year of 1868, the newly created Ollie L. Roberts would be 68 years of age in 1936, thus dishonestly qualifying for social security. I do believe this to be a logical theory of why Brushy changed his middle initial and birth year. Don't you agree?

Subsequent to Brushy changing his middle initial and birth year, I believe Brushy began constructing his Billy the Kid fantasy. In spite of his newly increased age, Brushy realized he would have been only 13 years of age when Billy the Kid was allegedly killed in 1881. Prior to his 1949 Morrison interviews, Brushy needed an earlier birth year for any possibility of his claim as Billy the Kid to be taken seriously. Within the Morrison interviews, Brushy reported his time of birth as the last hour of the last day of 1859 (December 31, 1859). This reported time of birth would yield an age appropriate for Billy the Kid. A person born December 31, 1859 would have been 21 years of age on that night in July 1881 when Pat Garrett reportedly killed Billy. This age also fits well with folklore and the accepted approximate age of Billy the Kid by most historians, researchers, and authors.

Brushy's two changes in birth years alone do not prove or disprove he was Oliver Pleasant Roberts. We do know Oliver Pleasant Roberts was born in 1879, not 1868 or 1859. We also know from public documents, Brushy used a form of the name Oliver Pleasant Roberts throughout his life. To believe Brushy was not Oliver would require acceptance of his fantastical fallacy of a 33 year old man accepted by Oliver's mother as her 13 year old *long lost son* to explain Brushy's use of Oliver's identity throughout his life. In believing this fabrication, one would also have to believe a young Ollie fled the safety of his parents' home in 1884 at the tender age of five. If you don't believe this *hogwash*, then Brushy was indeed Oliver Pleasant Roberts and the final birth year change is no more than a desperate effort by Brushy in search of a noteworthy legacy as Billy the Kid.

Brushy's Immediate Family. Henry Oliver Roberts Family (about 1895), Brushy (Oliver Pleasant Roberts) on far right, Henry Oliver Roberts on top left, Sara Elizabeth Ferguson Roberts in front of Henry Oliver. Photograph courtesy of Paul Emerson.

Brushy's Parents, Henry Oliver and Sara Elizabeth Ferguson Roberts. Photograph from about 1920, author's family collection.

Brushy's Fictional Genealogy

In the beginning of the chapter titled *Brushy Bill's Story* from *Alias Billy the Kid* (Sonnichsen, Morrison, 1955) based on the Morrison interviews, Brushy stated:

> "My grandfather, Ben Roberts, settled in Nacogdoches, Texas in 1835."
>
> "My mother's maiden name was Mary Adeline Dunn and her native state was Kentucky."
>
> "I was born at Buffalo Gap, December 31, 1859, the last hour of the last day of the year."
>
> "My real name is William Henry Roberts."
>
> "My father was J. H. Roberts."
>
> (Note: later in the interviews, Brushy referred to his father as "Wild Henry" Roberts).

A second transcription of the Morrison/Brushy taped interviews was performed by Mr. Fred Bean. His transcription indicated Brushy reported his father's name as James Henry Roberts.

Let's examine and analyze Brushy's utterances.

Brushy professed his father, J. H. Roberts or "Wild Henry" Roberts, was born March 8, 1832, eight miles from Lexington, Kentucky. His grandfather was allegedly Ben Roberts, settling in Nacogdoches, Texas in 1835. The first name of Brushy's stated father, James or John, is subject to debate due to different transcriptions of the Morrision/Brushy taped interviews. I believe Brushy meant James Henry Roberts, as I will discuss later. It doesn't really matter, however, since the names and genealogy are borrowed from an unrelated Roberts family (discussed in an upcoming chapter).

No records have been found of a J. H. Roberts married to a Mary Adeline Dunn, with a son, William Henry Roberts, born December 31, 1859 in Buffalo Gap, Texas; nor in the entire state of Texas. The obvious question is why Brushy would create a make-believe family complete with names and dates? The answer is twofold. Brushy required a birth year in the chronological vicinity of 1859 to be age appropriate for Billy the Kid in 1881. This manipulation also provided an acceptable explanation of why he used the name Ollie or Oliver in public records throughout his life.

As previously discussed, Brushy connected his fabricated Roberts family with his genuine Roberts family by creating a yarn of finding his dead cousin, Ollie, killed in a horse theft incident in about 1892. Brushy purported while returning Ollie's belongings to Ollie Roberts' family (Brushy's actual true family) in Sulphur Springs, Texas, he was accepted as a long lost son by Ollie's mother (Brushy's actual mother). In this same account, Brushy references a cousin, Martha, and her husband, Dudley Heath. As explained earlier, Martha was the daughter of Henry Oliver and Caroline Dunn Roberts while Oliver Pleasant Roberts (Ollie) was the son of Henry Oliver Roberts and his second wife, Sara Elizabeth Ferguson Roberts. With Martha and Ollie (Brushy) having the same father, Martha was actually Brushy's half sister, not his cousin.

Martha Vada Roberts Heath, Brushy's half sister he claimed was his cousin.
Photograph from the author's family collection.

Brushy stated his grandfather was Benjamin Roberts. This is false. Brushy's actual grandfather was Joseph Roberts, born 1797 in Virginia and died February 22, 1858 in Rusk County, Texas. Official records document the marriage of Joseph Roberts to Rachel Henson July 28, 1844 in Rusk County, Texas. The 4th born from this marriage was Brushy's father, Henry Oliver Roberts (b.1852, d.1924). It appears none of the Roberts' family Bibles or records have shown who the father of Henry Oliver Roberts was. Proof is substantial Henry Oliver's father was Joseph Roberts per an 1892 publication titled *A Memorial and Biographical History of Hill County, Texas.* Within this publication, the children of Joseph and Rachel Henson Roberts were named, including Henry Oliver Roberts, a resident of Hopkins County, Texas. It should be noted Sulphur Springs, Texas is in Hopkins County. The names of Henry Oliver's siblings concur exactly with my family's records, making it clear Joseph Roberts was indeed Oliver Pleasant Roberts' grandfather. From this, we can safely conclude Brushy's grandfather was Joseph, not Ben or Benjamin.

I introduced this chapter with a series of quotations by Brushy in regard to his genealogy. These statements are all false and completely fabricated. He did not have a father named John or James Henry Roberts, did not have a mother named Mary Adeline Dunn, did not have a birth name of William Henry Roberts, did not have a grandfather named Ben, and certainly was not born in Buffalo Gap, Texas on December 31, 1859. Brushy's actual birth name was indeed the identity he used throughout life in census, marriage, divorce, death certificates, and all public documents. His true name was Oliver Pleasant Roberts, son of Henry Oliver and Sara Elizabeth Ferguson Roberts, born August 26, 1879 in Bates, Arkansas.

I presume Brushy believers will not be satisfied with my conclusion as to Brushy's true identity. Their belief that Brushy was the actual historical Billy the Kid is so strong they will most likely ignore inconvenient facts and logic presented. However, if the reader is undecided regarding of the validity of Brushy's claim as Billy the Kid, many topic discussions remain dispelling even more elements of his fairy tale.

Pencil sketch of woman Brushy identified as his mother, Mary Adeline Dunn Roberts.
This sketch is actually Brushy's birth mother, Sara Elizabeth Ferguson Roberts.
Sketch by Linda Weatherman.

BRUSHY'S MOTHER MISINDENTIFICATION

On the preceding page, I have included a realistic pencil sketch of a photograph Brushy provided to Mr. Morrison during an interview. Unfortunately, due to copyright restrictions, I cannot provide the actual photograph in this book. The woman portrayed was identified by Brushy as his mother, Mary Adeline Dunn Roberts. However, the true identity of the person illustrated is evident after an August 1987 interview of Mr. William A. Tunstill with a family relative.

While conducting research for his book, Mr. Tunstill reported interviewing a member of the extended Roberts family. On page 35 of *Billy the Kid and Me Were the Same*, Tunstill included narrative from an interview with a lady he asserted was Brushy's second cousin. It appears this alleged second cousin wanted to remain unidentified, as her name was not revealed. Given Brushy (Oliver Pleasant Roberts) had many cousins, I unfortunately cannot determine for sure which individual this might have been. Considering Mr. Tunstill created much of the *Brushy believer* paranoia, I am actually surprised he included the content of this conversation. The statements by this relative in regard to picture identification do much to dispute Brushy's claim.

From his book, Mr. Tunstill states:

> My wife and I were invited to the home of Brushy Bill's second cousin. She said the first time she met Brushy Bill was when she was six years old. She visited her grandparents Henry Oliver and Sara Elizabeth Ferguson Roberts almost every summer until she was grown. They lived on a farm near Sulphur Springs, Texas.
>
> I brought some pictures with me and asked her to identify them if she could. All of them were Brushy Bill with

his attorney William V. Morrison, the second was with Governor Thomas Mabry. Yes, she said that's Ollie all right. Then she said, I want you and Mrs. Tunstill to see a picture of my grandmother, Sara Elizabeth Ferguson Roberts. We got up from our chairs and followed her to the living room. There on the wall was a large picture. I looked for about a minute and said I thought that was Brushy Bill's mother (Mary Adeline Dunn Roberts). Oh, no was her reply. I told her the same picture was illustrated on page 58 in the Sonnichsen/Morrison book, Alias Billy the Kid. This is a true fact. This is the only major mistake Brushy Bill made in the entire book. I know, I checked every page and every line in the entire book. As a matter of fact this picture was that of his aunt. Not bad for a ninety year old man to remember.

Let's evaluate Mr. Tunstill's statements. I have no reason to doubt the information provided by this supposed second cousin as accurate, but Tunstill's conclusion was all hogwash. When confronted with proper information from a Roberts family member, Mr. Tunstill intentionally detoured and denied reality.

Let's begin with the picture referenced (see page 29). Brushy previously identified the woman in the picture as his mother, Mary Adeline Dunn Roberts. Yes, the picture was indeed that of his mother, but was of Sara Elizabeth Ferguson Roberts, Brushy's birth mother and grandmother to the cousin Mr. Tunstill interviewed. When confronted with this correction of Brushy's lie, Mr. Tunstill admitted Brushy was wrong. However, instead of accepting the image as Brushy's biological mother, Tunstill went off into another tangent claiming the photo was of an aunt.

I found it strange that Mr. Tunstill decided this misidentification represented the *only* major mistake in Brushy's confabulated tale. A number of Brushy's falsehoods have been established up to this point with many more yet to follow. I also believe Mr. Tunstill became confused in regard to the second cousin identification. To be a second cousin, one must share a great-grandparent. Since the cousin interviewed referred to Henry Oliver and Sara Elizabeth Ferguson Roberts as her grandparents and we know they were the parents of Brushy (Oliver Pleasant Roberts), a second cousin relationship is incorrect. However, I do not doubt she was a relative, just not a second cousin. It's pure speculation, but I am inclined to believe she was the daughter of one of Brushy's siblings. In that case the proper term would have been niece. We all have to keep in mind Mr. Tunstill had his own unique way of determining family relationships departing significantly from accepted conventional standards.

How Did Brushy Derive His Paternal Genealogy

It now seems appropriate to discuss how Brushy derived his invented paternal genealogy. While it's possible he simply pulled names and dates out of thin air, I believe he borrowed names and dates for the creation of his make-believe genealogy from an unrelated Roberts family. During my research, I discovered records of a Roberts family with strong commonalities to Brushy's fabricated paternal family line.

Brushy purported his father's name was James Henry Roberts. He further stated his grandfather was Ben Roberts, settling in Nacogdoches, Texas in 1835. In my review of genealogical records, I discovered an unrelated Roberts family with these identical names. The James Henry Roberts family settled in the Nacogdoches, Texas vicinity. These records indicated a Benjamin Roberts (born around 1800) as the father of James Henry Roberts (b. 9/9/1839, d. 9/27/1893). James Henry Robert's son, William S. Roberts (born 5/1/1858), died in 1936 with his grave site in the Macedonia Cemetery in San Augustine County, Texas. Could there have been a younger sibling born in 1859 (Brushy's alleged year of birth) with a name of William Henry Roberts (Brushy's imaginary birth name)? No, of course there wasn't. I discovered a listing of all William S. Roberts' siblings and no William Henry Roberts is indicated. It should also be noted James Henry Roberts' wife was Cynthia Ann Causey, not Mary Adeline Dunn (Brushy's pretend birth mother). After an exhaustive search, I was unable to locate records supporting any actual Roberts family reflecting all of the names within Brushy's tale.

While the actual James Henry and Benjamin Roberts from the Nacogdoches, Texas vicinity were clearly not Brushy's father and grandfather, I believe Brushy used names, location, and approximate dates involving this Benjamin Roberts family for the creation of his fabricated family tree.

Although Brushy used the names of William, James Henry, and Benjamin Roberts in his fable, when selecting first and middle names for himself within his make-believe family, Brushy chose William Henry. Brushy's selectively fashioned name would then mirror aliases used by Billy the Kid of Henry McCarty, Henry Antrim, and William H. Bonney. Additionally, Brushy selected a birth year of 1859, the year believed by many to be the birth year of Billy the Kid. Brushy now had a complete imaginary paternal family line and proper age to support his claim as Billy the Kid.

Several authors have exhibited great effort in enhancing Brushy's imaginary genealogy even further. In a later chapter, I will discuss these false genealogical creations in detail.

Grave Headstone for William S. Roberts (b. 1858), Macedonia Cemetery, San Augustine, Texas. I believe this Roberts family represented a cornerstone for Brushy's fabricated family genealogy. William S. Roberts' father was James Henry Roberts. William S. Roberts' grandfather was Benjamin Roberts.

Historical accounts indicate Catherine McCarty produced two sons while living in New York: Henry McCarty, aka Billy the Kid, and Joseph McCarty. Although some debate exists whether Henry was the younger or older brother, most historians agree he was born in New York. In his interviews with Brushy, Mr. Morrison recognized two discrepancies requiring explanations.

The first problem to reconcile was the relationship between Brushy and Catherine McCarty, accepted by most historians as the mother of Billy the Kid. Brushy, however, while claiming to be Billy the Kid, stated his birth mother was Mary Adeline Dunn Roberts and Catherine McCarty was only his half aunt. How does Brushy account for this discrepancy? When asked by Mr. Morrison, Brushy explained folks only believed Catherine Bonney (McCarty Antrim) was his mother because that's what he told them.

The next departure from accepted historical accounts Brushy attempted to reconcile was his place of birth. Brushy declared his birthplace as Buffalo Gap, Texas. From the book *Alias Billy the Kid* (Sonnichsen, Morrison, 1955), it appears Mr. Morrison was aware of historical accounts indicating Henry McCarty's birthplace as New York. He asked Brushy the obvious question: "Do you know why they think Billy the Kid was born in New York?" Brushy replied, "I told Pat Garrett I was from New York. He never knew the difference. I never even knew where New York was located. I just heard someone say he was from New York one time so I used it myself."

Brushy stated his place of birth was Buffalo Gap, Texas, while most historical accounts indicate Henry McCarty, aka Billy the Kid, was born in New York. Catherine McCarty is well documented as residing in New York during the appropriate time of Henry's birth. Isn't it peculiar Brushy told others he was born in New York because "… I just heard someone say he was from New York one time so I used it myself?" I'm certainly not satisfied with his explanation, are you?

To further illustrate Brushy's place of birth problem, I am including a public document from the Department of the Interior (page 37) providing some clarification in regard to the issue. A questionnaire from the Department of the Interior was sent to Mr. William H. Antrim (stepfather of Henry McCarty, aka Billy the Kid) residing in El Paso, Texas. This form was for purposes of obtaining a military pension and was completed by Mr. Antrim April 2, 1915. Mr. Antrim stated his first marriage was to Catherine McCarty and indicated a previous marriage of Catherine to a Mr. McCarty who died in New York City. Mr. Antrim further stated Catherine had two sons. Historically, we know Catherine and her two sons resided in New York City until their move in 1867 to Indianapolis, Indiana. Historical accounts also show Catherine's two sons were Henry and Joseph carrying the last name of McCarty. In addition, Mr. Antrim related one of Catherine's sons died in the eighties and the other he had not heard from in 14 years.

Assuming William H. Antrim provided correct information on the government document (see page 37), we can derive some interesting scenarios. First, since the information Mr. Antrim provided is consistent with known facts, it appears conclusive this Mr. Antrim was certainly Henry McCarty's (Billy the Kid's) stepfather. Secondly, Mr. Antrim reported Catherine's first husband, Mr. McCarty, died in New York City. New York represents a city that was home to Catherine and her boys for a number of years and the place of death of a man whose last name Catherine, Henry, and Joseph all carried. Yet, Brushy asserted never hearing of New York until someone mentioned the place to him in passing. Brushy further stated folks just thought he was from New York because he lied by telling them he was. I find it difficult to believe Brushy had never heard of his namesake's place of death and his home town for a number of years. From the preponderance of evidence, I believe historical accounts of Henry McCarty, aka Billy the Kid, and his brother, Joseph, were born in New York as correct. It would also appear the brothers were both products of the McCarty marriage. This conflicts with Brushy's claim of birth in Buffalo Gap, Texas, his mother as the nonexistent Mary Adeline Dunn, and father as the imaginary James Henry Roberts.

Finally, Mr. Antrim's statement (see item 9 on page 37) one son "died in the '80s" and the other "he had not heard from in 14 years" (preceding the document date of 1915) is incredibly enlightening. Research supports

Joseph McCarty Antrim's (believed to be Henry's brother) death as November 25, 1930 in Denver, Colorado. This leaves us with the other son dying in the 1880s. Remember, Henry McCarty, aka Billy the Kid, was allegedly killed by Pat Garrett July 14, 1881. 1881 is certainly in the '80s. Is this a coincidence?

While constructing his fable, Brushy was obviously aware of Billy the Kid history and folklore. With any serious probing, he would certainly be questioned regarding birth mother and birthplace discrepancies. In light of Mr. Antrim's written statements, I believe you will find Brushy's explanations not logically satisfying. But, since Brushy was actually Oliver Pleasant Roberts, still living with his parents in Sulphur Springs, Texas beyond the age of 20, I don't believe any explanation he provided would satisfy logical scrutiny.

William H. Antrim (Billy the Kid's Stepfather), 1858-1918.
Brushy claimed Antrim was his half aunt's husband.

3—389

DEPARTMENT OF THE INTERIOR
BUREAU OF PENSIONS

WASHINGTON, D. C., *January 2, 1915.*

SIR: Please answer, at your earliest convenience, the questions enumerated below. The information is requested for future use, and it may be of great value to your widow or children. Use the inclosed envelope, which requires no stamp.

Very respectfully,

G M Saltzgaber

Commissioner.

WILLIAM H ANTRIM
EL PASO TEX
977482   ACT MAY
HOTEL DELMAR

No. 1. Date and place of birth? *Answer.* 1st day of December 1842 Huntsville Ind

The name of organizations in which you served? *Answer.* Co. I and vol 54th Ind vols

No. 2. What was your post office at enlistment? *Answer.* Indianaplis Ind

No. 3. State your wife's full name and her maiden name. *Answer.* Cathrine Antrim

No. 4. When, where, and by whom were you married? *Answer.* Santafe New mexico in the later part of 1872 or first part of 1873

No. 5. Is there any official or church record of your marriage? Was maried in Presbyterian Church

If so, where? *Answer.* at santafe I think it is on record in Church —

No. 6. Were you previously married? If so, state the name of your former wife, the date of the marriage, and the date and place of her death or divorce. If there was more than one previous marriage, let your answer include all former wives. *Answer.* Was not maried the first

No. 7. If your present wife was married before her marriage to you, state the name of her former husband, the date of such marriage, and the date and place of his death or divorce, and state whether he ever rendered any military or naval service, and, if so, give name of the organization in which he served. If she was married more than once before her marriage to you, let your answer include all former husbands. *Answer.* This is not of my own knowledge she was maried to McCarty date not noen - died in New york City date not noen no other marage no military service that I no of

No. 8. Are you now living with your wife, or has there been a separation? *Answer.* my Wife died Night the 13th of Sept 18-74 of tarhue Robusus in Silber City

No. 9. State the names and dates of birth of all your children, living or dead. *Answer.* She had no children my Wife had two Boys one died in the eighteys & the other I have not herd from in 14teen years

Date April 2st 1915   (Signature) William H. Antrim

Application for Military Pension.

FALSE GENEALOGICAL LEAPS BY AUTHORS

After considerable disproof of Brushy's identity claim as Henry McCarty, aka Billy the Kid, I now examine false leaps in genealogical connections by authors enhancing Brushy's stated ancestry. I will discuss how both Brushy and authors deceitfully intertwine Henry McCarty with the Roberts family heritage.

Historians agree Henry's mother was Catherine McCarty Antrim. Considerable debate remains whether she ever carried the last name of Bonney as stated by Brushy. Although some believe Bonney was Catherine's maiden name, others presume it was from a first marriage, while many historians conclude the Bonney name completely unrelated. All we know for certain in regard to the Bonney name is Henry McCarty, aka Billy the Kid, used the alias William H. Bonney. Historians do agree Henry's mother, Catherine McCarty, later remarried assuming the last name Antrim. In the Morrison interviews, Brushy stated his half aunt was Catherine Bonney McCarty, later becoming Catherine Antrim.

One interesting piece of evidence indicating the Bonney name was not due to a prior marriage of Catherine is the previously referred document from the Department of the Interior completed by William H. Antrim dated April 2, 1915. The purpose of the document was to obtain a military pension (see page 37). Mr. Antrim stated his wife was Catherine Antrim. They married in Santa Fe, New Mexico, and she died September 13, 1874 from tuberculosis. One item on the form asks if his wife was married earlier and if so, to list any former husbands. Mr. Antrim wrote, "She was married to McCarty date not known, died in New York City, date not known, no other marriage." Assuming Mr. Antrim's memory was not faulty at the age of 72, Catherine had never possessed the name of Bonney due to marriage. This evidence would imply that if she ever carried the Bonney name, it was her maiden last name.

Although Bonney could have possibly been Catherine's maiden name, Mr. Tunstill, in his book *Billy the Kid And Me Were the Same*, presumed this unproven maiden name as fact. In his pseudo-history book, he creatively connected my Roberts family to the Bonney name. Mr. Tunstill proclaimed knowing intimate knowledge of my great-great-great-grandmother Eva Talitha Counts Dunn (although he certainly did not know her name). Mr. Tunstill declared she was the Cherokee wife of a Mr. Bonney and produced a child named Catherine Bonney. It's quite amazing how Mr. Tunstill could have such knowledge considering he did not even know her name, or know her first husband's name other than he was a Mr. Bonney. Once again, Mr. Tunstill confabulated unfounded and false connections in my family necessary to fit with Brushy's claims, including Catherine as his half aunt.

These giant false leaps in genealogical connections by Mr. Tunstill were well summarized by Mr. W. C. Jameson. On pages 89 and 91 of the paperback version of W. C. Jameson's book titled *The Return of the Outlaw Billy the Kid* published in 1998, he states:

> The origin of the name Bonney has long eluded and confused Billy the Kid researchers; they have never been able to learn where it came from. Roberts had an answer, and his claims have subsequently been supported by a genealogy taken from the family Bible of the late Texas resident Martha Vada Roberts Heath. Heath was the daughter of Henry Oliver Roberts (brother to James Henry Roberts) and Caroline Dunn (sister to Mary Adeline Dunn). According to genealogy records provided to the authors by Heath descendants and researcher William A. Tunstill, William Henry Roberts' aunt Catherine Bonney (b. 1829) was the daughter of a man named Bonney (first name unknown) and an unnamed wife. Following the death of Bonney, the wife married William Dunn and the two begat Mary Adeline, Catherine Bonney's half sister.

The above stated relationship between my family's Caroline Dunn and the imaginary Mary Adeline Dunn was reported in the book published in 1988 by William Tunstill titled *Billy the Kid and Me Were the Same*. My great-great-grandfather, Henry Oliver Roberts, was falsely indicated in the above excerpt as a brother to fictional James Henry Roberts. Mr. Tunstill stated this family genealogy was supported in a Heath Family Bible. I do not believe either claim is supported by entries in my great-grandmother's Heath family Bible. If so, I would certainly like to inspect how it had been falsified. In reality, I do not believe anything was actually falsified in a Heath family Bible. I am quite certain Mr. Tunstill, in his enthusiasm to publish a history alteration book, simply fabricated details to suit his needs. The claims of Caroline Dunn having a sister named Mary Adeline Dunn, and of Henry Oliver Roberts having a brother named James Henry Roberts (or J. H. Roberts) are both absolute fiction.

Throughout his interviews with Morrison, Brushy never indicated a sibling relationship between his pretend father, James Henry Roberts, and his actual father, Henry Oliver Roberts. The brother relationship was completely fabricated by Mr. Tunstill and repeated by subsequent Brushy believer authors, including Mr. Jameson. While Brushy identified his actual half sister Martha Roberts Heath as cousin Martha, Mr. Tunstill jumped to the conclusion nonexistent James Henry was Henry Oliver's brother with a common make-believe father, Benjamin. In fact, Henry Oliver Roberts' documented father was Joseph Roberts, not Ben or Benjamin Roberts.

It is clear Brushy used the cousin Martha term due to a kinship on his maternal side. Martha Vada's mother was Caroline Dunn, the first wife of Henry Oliver Roberts. Brushy attempted connecting Caroline Dunn with his imaginary mother, Mary Adeline Dunn. It is true Caroline had a sister named Mary, but no middle name of Adeline. This Mary did not wed Brushy's fictional father, James Henry Roberts (she married to become Mary Bruton). A Nancy Adeline Dunn did exist in our family, but the last name of Dunn was a result of a marriage to Caroline Dunn's half brother. I suspect Brushy used a portion of the two names in deriving the fanciful name Mary Adeline Dunn as his mother. As we know by now, it was not uncommon for Brushy to use variations and portions of actual Roberts' family names within his story creations.

Brushy maintained Catherine Bonney (McCarty, Antrim) was his half aunt. If this had been true, it would represent an alteration from historical accounts indicating Catherine McCarty Antrim as the mother of Henry McCarty, aka Billy the Kid. Brushy's claim of half aunt Catherine McCarty Antrim raising him in Silver City, New Mexico did, however, provide a necessary connection to her for any hope of his fable to be believed. Both accurate and inaccurate accounts of Billy the Kid agree Catherine and young Henry were together in Silver City, New Mexico at the same time.

In composing his book, Mr. Tunstill consulted with my mother, Eulaine Haws, great-granddaughter of Henry Oliver Roberts (Brushy's actual father). After reviewing numerous pieces of correspondence between Mr. Tunstill and my mother, I now realize how she mistakenly aided Mr. Tunstill by acknowledging the false genealogy provided her. In the early 1980s, Mr. Tunstill communicated often with her over a period of five years. During this period of time, he successfully convinced my mother of the validity of his false Roberts family genealogical creations. Unfortunately, she believed Mr. Tunstill, agreeing without substantiated proof. In this way, Mr. Tunstill secured a Roberts family acknowledgment of his imaginative key genealogical connections. These included a fabricated sister relationship between Caroline Dunn Roberts and Brushy's invented mother, Mary Adeline Dunn Roberts; and support of a half sister relationship of Caroline and fictional Mary Adeline with Catherine Bonney (McCarty, Antrim). For overkill, Mr. Tunstill then fashioned a sibling relationship between Brushy's actual father, Henry Oliver Roberts, and his imaginary father, James Henry Roberts. For unknown reasons, Mr. Tunstill deemed this enhancement necessary to further supplement Brushy's fable.

With a Roberts family member's acknowledgment supporting his false genealogical fabrications, Mr. Tunstill now had a basis for his absurd book, *Billy the Kid And Me Were the Same*. I consider the categorization of Mr. Tunstill's book as non-fiction highly unfortunate. It was particularly deplorable as Tunstill's false Roberts family genealogy creations were readily accepted as fact by subsequent book authors bitten by the Brushy believer phenomenon.

To further illustrate circumstances surrounding how Mr. Tunstill duped my mother, Eulaine Haws, into family acknowledgment of his unfounded genealogy, I include an excerpt from her notes summarizing her association with Mr. Tunstill:

> The phone rang. I answered it and a voice asked, "Are you Eulaine Haws?" "Yes," I answered. "Was your grandmother, Martha Roberts Heath?" the voice asked. "Yes", I answered. "Then, I think you are a cousin of Brushy Bill Roberts, known as Billy the Kid," he replied. "Oh no, you're joking." was my reply. Well, that was the shock of my life that turned out to be true. I now have a family tree chart. It seems that my grandmother's death certificate contained her mother's maiden name of Dunn. Her step-mother and father had helped raise Billy for several years and claimed him as their son to protect him from the law. My grandmother even called him brother. I now have proof that Brushy Bill Roberts, alias Billy the Kid, of Hico, Texas, is my double third cousin. Mr. Tunstill has worked on research for Brushy Bill for about eight years. I have helped him for the last five years.

During the early 1980s, my mother, Eulaine Haws, continued conversing and corresponding on many occasions with Mr. Tunstill. I am in possession of many pieces of correspondence between my mother and Mr. Tunstill. It was interesting how his *selling job* with false genealogy and theories progressed over time. My mother's enthusiasm over the project was so strong, she purchased a considerable number of copies of his pseudo-history book and tended to give them away to anyone who would take one, especially since her name was now in print as a relative of Billy the Kid.. On page 37 of his book, *Billy the Kid And Me Were The Same*, Mr. Tunstill included one of the many letters she wrote him:

> July 14, 1983
> Dear Mr. Tunstill,
> I enjoyed your call last night very much. Martha

Roberts Heath was my grandmother, so that makes Henry Oliver Roberts my great-grandfather and Benjamin Roberts my great-great-grandfather. O. L. (Oliver or Ollie or Brushy Bill) was my grandmother's first cousin, so that would make me his third cousin.

From your research, I believe he was the real Billy the Kid. You certainly have my permission to change the tombstone at your own expense. I think you said it was listed as William Henry Roberts on the stone.

I was not fortunate enough to meet this cousin, but my brother Paul Emerson did. He was rather small but remembers him claiming to be "The Kid." He says he was a "cocky" guy and he liked his story but no one else seemed to believe him. Paul and my mother, Vada Bell Heath Emerson, lived next door to my grandmother, Martha Roberts Heath, for several years and took care of her. She and her husband, Monroe Dudley Heath, are buried in the Old Palestine cemetery near Alto, Texas.

I wish you the best of luck with the rest of your research project. I have enjoyed your letters, and if there is anything else I can do to help you, I will be happy to do so. I will get in touch with my cousin, Henry Heath, and his wife, Joe, as soon as possible.

Sincerely,

Eulaine Haws

Yes, my mother's grandmother, Martha Vada Roberts Heath, had good reason to call Brushy her brother. Brushy was, in fact, her half brother, Oliver Pleasant Roberts. Brushy was actually the half granduncle of my mother, Eulaine Haws, while Mr. Tunstill insisted he was her double third cousin. I do not believe Roberts' family genealogical records exist in a Heath Family Bible reflecting Roberts' family ancestors prior to Henry Oliver Roberts. From the correspondence between Mr. Tunstill and my mother, I also know the Heath Family Bible referred to was in the possession of a relative and was unavailable for review by Mr. Tunstill. As discussed earlier, my research has clearly shown Henry Oliver's father was Joseph, not Benjamin; therefore, this connection of my family to a fictional ancestor named Benjamin Roberts was falsely provided by Mr. Tunstill. This fabricated genealogical creation served him well in his misguided attempt to validate Brushy's report of a grandfather named Ben.

Mr. Tunstill's groundless leap declaring Caroline Dunn Roberts (first wife of Henry Oliver Roberts) as the sister of nonexistent Mary Adeline Dunn Roberts (Brushy's imaginary mother) was necessary to support Brushy's saga. Records do not exist of a Mary Adeline Dunn related to my Roberts family. The invalidly constructed Roberts family tree additionally depicts this same fictional Mary Adeline Dunn as married to the fictional James Henry Roberts (or J. H. Roberts or *Wild* Henry Roberts). This fabricated marriage of two fictional individuals yielded a fictional son, William Henry Roberts, the name Brushy professed was his at birth. Can you now see how Mr. Tunstill's cleverly crafted genealogy supported Brushy's fantasy?

Since all of this was perhaps difficult to follow and at the expense of becoming repetitive, I will summarize Mr. Tunstill's phony genealogical connections of Caroline Dunn and nonexistent Mary Adeline Dunn (Brushy's claimed mother) to Catherine McCarty Antrim (mother of Henry McCarty, aka Billy the Kid). He identified the fictitious Mary Adeline Dunn and Caroline Dunn (first wife of Henry Oliver Roberts), as the children of a Mr. Dunn and a Cherokee woman (her second marriage, but name unknown). Mr. Tunstill further contended this same Cherokee woman's first marriage was to a Mr. Bonney, yielding a daughter named Catherine Bonney (Mr. Tunstill spelled Catherine as Katherine). Mr. Tunstill conveniently proclaimed knowledge of Caroline Dunn's mother having a mysterious first marriage to a Mr. Bonney. This unfounded opportune marriage produced Catherine Bonney, thus satisfying Brushy's claim of Catherine as his half aunt. In contrast to Mr. Tunstill's claims, my research found Caroline Dunn as the child of Francis Dunn and Eva Talitha Counts. Although Eva's heritage is unknown, no evidence exists of a prior marriage to a Mr. Bonney.

Certain authors and historians believe Catherine McCarty Antrim, the mother of Henry McCarty, aka Billy the Kid, at one time held the last name of Bonney (either as maiden or by marriage). As stated earlier, considerable debate and controversy continues regarding the Bonney name. We do know, however, Mr. William H. Antrim (Catherine's second husband) stated in a government document (see page 37) Catherine had no husband before McCarty. There is certainly no documented proof indicating Catherine ever carried the last name of Bonney. In spite of continuing controversy, Mr. Tunstill considered Catherine's maiden name as Bonney (daughter of a Cherokee wife and an unknown Mr. Bonney) factual in his undaunted desire of supporting Brushy's false claim of a genealogical connection to Catherine. Author creativity can never be underestimated.

Complicated Fake Family Tree from Tunstill's Press Release, 1990. It was designed by Eulaine Haws from false genealogy provided by William A. Tunstill.

Interestingly, although Mr. Tunstill referenced the aforementioned genealogical connections, he did not include the falsely crafted Roberts family tree in his book *Billy the Kid and Me Were the Same*. I have included it on the previous page for your review. This chart was a media press release by Mr. Tunstill in 1990. This complicatedly drawn, unsupported Roberts family tree (designed by my mother, Eulaine Haws, using key false genealogical connections provided by Mr. Tunstill) is absolute fiction engineered entirely for purposes of enhancing Brushy's great hoax.

My actual Roberts family tree on my maternal side, however, is much simpler. Below you will see an abbreviated version showing pertinent individuals and their known relationships.

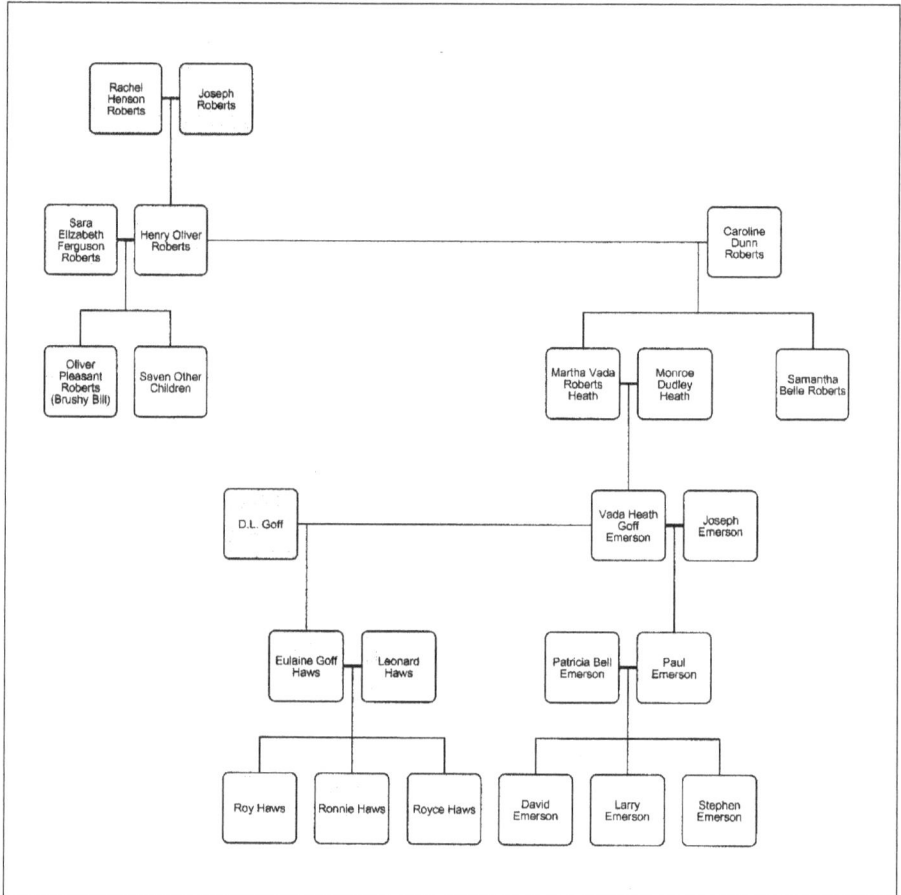

In his desire to publish a fascinating narrative, Mr. Tunstill committed a series of errors beginning with the false premise Brushy's statements in the Morrison interviews were indeed factual. Mr. Tunstill proceeded to substantiate Brushy as the famous outlaw by manipulating construction of a purely imaginative family tree, not only accommodating Brushy's story, but enhancing it. In order to add to the validity of false and unsupported genealogy, Mr. Tunstill utilized my mother, Eulaine Haws, for family acknowledgment of his false genealogical creations. Further confusing the general public, subsequent authors, including W. C. Jameson, employed Tunstill's false Roberts family genealogy. In conjunction with Brushy's imaginative narrative, authors then had a ground floor basis for their pseudo-history creations. I consider this incredibly unfortunate as it birthed large numbers of *Brushy believers*. Over the years, the *Brushy believer hoax* phenomenon has propagated much like a computer virus or worm.

Gravestone of Brushy's Parents, Henry Oliver and Sara Elizabeth Ferguson Roberts. Hillcrest Cemetery, Canton, Texas. Photograph provided by Barbara Martin Haws.

Genealogical Error by Brushy

With so many names, dates, family relationships, and events for Brushy to keep straight, errors occurred damaging his tale. As with many myths, blending facts with fiction often creates unexplainable mistakes. For Brushy, it was no exception. According to Brushy, his imaginary mother, Mary Adeline Dunn Roberts, died when he was less than three years of age. He reported a second marriage of his fictional father, James Henry Roberts. A gigantic mistake by Brushy occurred when reporting his imaginary father marrying a woman named Elizabeth Ferguson.

Brushy reported remaining with his "father" and "step-mother," Elizabeth, for only two years. In the book *Alias Billy the Kid* (Morrison, Sonnichsen, 1955), it was stated, "Brushy consistently called his father's second wife Mother."

Why would Brushy identify an imaginary step-mother as his mother when he had avouched knowing her only a short time? This was especially true in the case of his fantasied step-mother who possessed the same name as his true birth mother. Actually, the statement of Brushy referring to his make-believe step-mother, Elizabeth Ferguson, as mother is understandable since Sara Elizabeth Ferguson Roberts was Brushy's biological mother. Sara Elizabeth Ferguson was the second wife of Brushy's true father, Henry Oliver Roberts. Sara Elizabeth gave birth August 26, 1879 to Oliver Pleasant Roberts who is, of course, Brushy. However, in his statement, Brushy is referring to the second wife of his make-believe father, James Henry Roberts. It appears Brushy found difficulty keeping his true family relationships out of conflict with those he fabricated. In his attempt to blend his pretend family line with his own well documented true family, he failed miserably.

How do believer authors rectify or attempt to explain this huge error? Some have simply breezed past this rather inconvenient error by ignoring it.

Other authors describe it as a Morrison transcription error or a verbal mistake by Brushy. Still others have assumed Henry Oliver Roberts and nonexistent James Henry Roberts had the same second wife or perhaps married ladies with the same name. Of course, the Brushy believers have adopted one or more of the above-mentioned excuses to accommodate this seemingly irreconcilable difficulty.

It appears Brushy believer authors have shown incredible usage of any stretch of imagination accommodating Brushy's bunk. They have included any portion of Brushy's fibbery reasonably consistent with historical accounts, yet carefully excluded obvious falsehoods and inconsistencies. After all, fantastic stories sell books and drive the Brushy believer paranoia. What could be better than a work of imagination of an infamous character of the Old West supposedly killed in 1881, later resurfacing to have lived a long life of over 90 years into the mid-20th century?

Three of the "Brushy Believer" Authors All Together.
Left to right: Dr. Jannay P. Valdez, Judge Bobby Hefner, William A. Tunstill.
Photograph from the Eulaine Haws collection.

Brushy, William Henry, and Ollie (all the same)

Brushy alleged using a number of aliases before, during, and after the Lincoln County War in New Mexico. He maintained using new monikers after 1881 for obvious reasons. Since no one knew Brushy by his alleged birth name of William Henry Roberts, why didn't he just revert to this name? Public records have not been found with Brushy's usage of his claimed birth name. Of course, Brushy had an explanation for never using his nonexistent birth name of William Henry Roberts.

In the book *Alias Billy the Kid* (Morrison, Sonnichsen, 1955), it was stated: "His real name was William Henry Roberts. At the age of three he changed it for what seemed adequate reason." Then later in the Morrison interviews, Brushy stated, "I left that home (his alleged father's) as soon as I was well enough to travel, which was in May of 1874. That's when I quit using my real name, too. Never went back to using William Henry Roberts until last year (1949) when you found me."

Brushy said he discontinued using his alleged birth name of William Henry Roberts at the age of fourteen, yet earlier in the Morrison interviews, he said he changed it at the age of three. It's a bit hard to imagine a child of three changing his own name. The age of fourteen certainly makes more sense than the age three, yet shows considerable inconsistency in Brushy's narrative.

As previously discussed, public records do not support a person named William Henry Roberts born on December 31, 1859 in Buffalo Gap, Texas. Additionally, in searching all available Texas public records and Roberts family genealogy, no family can be found which includes William Henry Roberts, James Henry Roberts (or J. H. Roberts), and Mary Adeline Dunn in the entire state of Texas during this time period. This is a completely nonexistent family concocted entirely for use in Brushy's tall tale.

At this point, I believe all open-minded readers should now at least be convinced Brushy's true name was not William Henry Roberts, but perhaps still need more evidence to prove he wasn't Billy the Kid. For those not yet convinced of Brushy's true identity and his story as a make-believe tale, please read on. The next chapter should prove enlightening as to what members of my extended family thought regarding Brushy's identity and his imaginative yarns.

Pencil sketch of Brushy. Artwork by Linda Weatherman.

WHAT THE FAMILY THOUGHT OF BRUSHY

One piece of family input supporting the conclusion Brushy was actually Oliver Pleasant Roberts is a handwritten letter dated December 6, 1987 by Mrs. Geneva Pittmon (b.1918, d.2008). Her grandparents were Henry Oliver Roberts and his second wife, Sara Elizabeth Ferguson. Mrs. Geneva Pittmon was the daughter of Oliver Pleasant Roberts' brother, Thomas Ulce Roberts. Thomas, known as Tom, knew his brother Brushy throughout his life. Brushy (Oliver) and Tom continued to live with their parents after they moved from Hopkins County to Van Zandt County, until the early 1900s. In her letter, Mrs. Geneva Pittmon clearly stated her Uncle Brushy was Oliver P. Roberts and not Billy the Kid. Mrs. Pittmon, born in 1918, reported knowing her Uncle Brushy (Oliver) well. Following is the complete content of her letter written to the Billy the Kid Gang founder, Joe Bowlin. The letter content has been reprinted by other authors including Jim Johnson from his book titled *Billy the Kid, His Real Name Was ...* (Outskirts Press, 2006.) The letter reads as follows:

December 16, 1987

Dear Sir: The reason you are not finding my family is you don't have the right name. My grandfather was H. O. Roberts married to Sara Elizabeth Ferguson on May 14, 1876. Oliver P. Roberts was Brushy Bill's name. I don't know what the P. was for. He was born August 26, 1879. I have the family Bible record. My husband thinks I should not tell you anything unless I know what your interests are in my family. A William A. Tunstill, P O Box 995, Roswell, New Mexico 88201 is also writing me asking questions which I have not written. He also has come up with a Ben Roberts as my great grandfather who was from (Kentucky?) and settled near Austin, 1835. I would also like for this to be settled as I know my Uncle Oliver was not Billy the Kid.

Mrs. Geneva Pittmon

To my knowledge, my only living relative who actually met Brushy (Oliver Pleasant Roberts) is my half uncle, Paul Emerson, of Houston, Texas. Paul related in a March 31, 2014 email, he was a teenager of about 16 years of age when Brushy visited the home of his grandmother, Martha Vada Heath (Brushy's half sister), in Jacksonville, Texas. My half uncle Paul believes the visit was in 1946 or 1947. Here is the pertinent excerpt from his email:

> I don't remember for sure just how old I was when Brushy (Oliver) came to see grandmother. I could have been a little older than 16, and we all knew he claimed to be Billy the Kid. Grandmother was glad to see him and he was nice. He was a small man (if I remember correctly), not too tall and he wore his cowboy clothes, boots, etc. I don't recall him coming over to our house, but it's possible he did. But I do remember grandmother saying he was not Billy the Kid. I think Eulaine and my boys really wanted him to be whether he was or not.
>
> Paul Emerson

Note: In the above email excerpt, the Eulaine referenced was my mother, Eulaine Haws, who passed away in January, 2005. Brushy's Jacksonville, Texas visit was with his half sister, Martha Vada Roberts Heath. At the time of Brushy's visit, Eulaine's half brother, Paul Emerson, was still living at home with his (and Eulaine's) mother, Vada Bell Heath Emerson (daughter of Martha Vada Roberts Heath). Their house was next door to their grandmother, Martha Vada Roberts Heath (widow of Dudley Heath). In interviews with Morrison, Brushy mentioned his cousin, Martha, in addition to her husband, Dudley Heath. I will state again, Martha Vada Roberts Heath was not Brushy's cousin; she was, in fact, his half sister.

In searching through my mother's papers and correspondence, I discovered a detailed letter written by my half uncle, Paul Emerson, to Mr. William Tunstill. He sent a copy of this letter to my mother since she requested he write Mr. Tunstill. The letter was dated August 2, 1986 and addressed to Mr. William A. Tunstill of Roswell, New Mexico. The complete content of this letter is as follows:

Dear Mr. Tunstill:

I have read your letters and the articles you have sent my sister, Eulaine Haws, about Oliver (Brushy Bill) Roberts, who said he was Billy the Kid. You have certainly done a lot of research and worked hard and I find it very interesting and fascinating to say the least. I remember meeting Oliver Roberts, who was my grandmother's brother, not too long before my grandmother died. She was Martha Vada Roberts Heath and was my mother's mother. Oliver came to see her in Jacksonville, Texas, and I met him. He was a very "dikey" little man that paraded around in western clothes and cowboy boots, and said he was Billy the Kid. I wish I would have listened more carefully to what he had to say, spent more time in his presence, and got him to tell me some of his stories; but I was young and too busy, I guess.

To be honest, my grandmother did not believe he was Billy the Kid and did not have confidence in what he said. She thought it was in the imagination of his mind. I do not personally know.

I am enclosing a copy of the newspaper clipping about his death that I found in my mother's papers after her death. On the back is a note written by my aunt Cora Heath, Martha Roberts Heath's second oldest daughter. She said: "O. L. Roberts was my mother's brother. He was around 75 years of age when he died and he was not Billy the Kid." I feel sure she expressed the sentiment of my grandmother about the subject. If Oliver was really her cousin and not her brother as the theory goes, she did not know it, or ever tell it to any of the children. I lived next door to my grandmother for a number of years in her older days, and her mind was very sharp until the day of her death. She was a person that talked about her family and her children to everyone sparing nothing, but I never remember hearing her say or express at any time that Oliver was not her brother. She just discounted what he said as a "state of mind."

I called and talked to Uncle Tom Roberts' daughter, Geneva Pittmon of Canton, Texas tonight. There are several direct nieces and nephews of Oliver Roberts still living which would be a generation closer than my sister Eulaine and I. Geneva told me that a couple of years ago, a reporter from the *Dallas News* came down and took pictures, interviewed them and ran a big article in the papers about it. She remembered your name but just what connection or contact with you she had, she did not say.

Mr. Tunstill, I do not wish to deflate any effort on your part to prove that Oliver (Ollie) (Brushy Bill) Roberts was Billy the Kid, but she said emphatically, without doubt or question, maybe, or don't know ... that it was not so. She says they have documents, papers, etc., to prove it is not so. She says that Oliver lived with her family a number of years throughout her life as a girl growing up. She remembers him quite well, has pictures of him, and knows very much about him. So, in light of the fact that Uncle Tom Roberts' children knew him, it would be good and better to contact them for most all the information you need. They have the family records. I suppose the Bible and pictures, etc., of him.

I wish I could be of more help, but I only saw him once and know very little about him. I have three sons and they would like very much for him to be the real genuine Billy the Kid. It really does not matter to me either way, but I would want, as I am sure you want, only the truth known. I wouldn't want to claim something that was not true. If I remember correctly, Billy the Kid was supposedly killed in 1881, but Oliver was only two years old at the time, being born in 1879. How can you reconcile the big age difference, and when did he switch persons.

Tom was younger than Oliver and, of course knew his brother. When Oliver would be gone for a time or get sick, he would always call his brother Tom to come, and Tom would go and see about him, Geneva said. I am sure Tom would have known if it was not his own brother. Well, whatever, but just please do contact her and other members of her family that knew and remembered Oliver quite well. They can fill you in on a lot of fact. Ok?

With best personal regards from us, and a prayer that God will bless you, I am,

Sincerely yours,

Paul Emerson, grandson of Martha Vada Roberts Heath

Paul Emerson and Vada Bell Heath Emerson (daughter of Martha Vada Roberts Heath). Courtesy of the author's family collection.

As I understood my half uncle, Paul Emerson, and my mother, Eulaine Haws, no one in our family truly initially believed Brushy (Oliver Pleasant Roberts) was Billy the Kid. Unfortunately, my mother was convinced otherwise after provided fabricated genealogy by Mr. Tunstill. My family knew Brushy was the nickname Oliver used through much of his life. Substantial time was spent with him by various family members throughout his life.

As we know, it is not uncommon for a family to have a relative with a creative imagination telling *tall tales* filled with fantastical exaggeration. I believe our family just thought my maternal half great-granduncle, Brushy (Oliver Pleasant Roberts), was an entertaining storyteller. Without the aid of creative authors, I believe Brushy's stories would have remained as little more than family footnotes.

Although information from my family in regard to Brushy should have been sufficient enough to dispel anyone's belief he was Billy the Kid, Mr. Tunstill continued to *plow on* in his attempt to prove his impossible theory. This required genealogical fabrications, pseudo-history, false witness testimonials, and intentional exclusion of obvious falsehoods in Brushy's *tall tale*.

It appears Brushy concocted his Billy the Kid *myth* before leaving Gladewater, Texas in about 1942. After relocating to Hamilton County, Texas, living in either Hamilton, Texas or Hico, Texas during the remainder of his life, it appears he would readily tell of his imagined escapades to anyone who would listen.

Still not convinced Brushy was just a colorful storyteller? The next chapter will provide some insight into what local residents thought of Brushy and his fables. While reading, please keep in mind Brushy professed he hadn't told anyone he was Billy the Kid prior to his interviews with Morrison in 1949.

Eulaine Haws and Paul Emerson. 1975 photograph of the author's mother and uncle. They are the children of Vada Bell Heath Emerson and grandchildren of Martha Vada Roberts Heath. Their great-grandfather was Henry Oliver Roberts, father of Brushy. Courtesy of the author's family collection.

What a Hamilton Resident Thought of Brushy

From my research, I discovered an interesting testimonial from Mrs. Elreeta Weathers as published in 1998 in her on-line publication *People and Places: Gazetteer of Hamilton County, Texas (Weathers, "Brushy Bill or Billy the Kid?").(http://freepages.genealogy.rootsweb.ancestry. com/~gazetteer2000/b/brushy_b.htm)*

Mrs. Elreeta Weathers' statement reads as follows:

> I don't know anything about the validity of Brushy Bill's claims to his being Billy the Kid, because I have not studied them.
>
> I do remember that he was a wiry little man, whom I thought was crazy. Mother and I would do everything we could to avoid being trapped by Brushy Bill, as we knew him. In retrospect, I would now classify his behavior as a form of dementia. We did not believe most of his claims and did not like to be the audience for his rantings and ravings. We pitied the other poor souls whom he did trap.
>
> Roberts would "trap" people between himself and one of the light posts around the square. Once someone was "trapped", Brushy Bill would begin his tirade about his being Billy the Kid, displaying his small wrists and explaining how he had once slipped out of a pair of handcuffs to escape. He also told us that he made his own shirt ... and either he or Mrs. Roberts obviously did. His shirts were always constructed of brightly colored and patterned fabric. At that time it was not possible to buy shirts made with such designs. The shirts were likely made from quadrica, a broadcloth-type fabric available at that time. The diminutive, mustached Mr. Roberts always wore a western hat and tied a red kerchief around his neck. Mr. Roberts died while I was in high school.

Mrs. Elreeta Weathers

Brushy moved from Gladewater, Texas to Hamilton County, Texas in about 1942. Based on my conversations with Mrs. Weathers, her recollections were from the latter 1940s. This would be at a time after Brushy began using the name O. L. Roberts and was married to Malinda Allison. Mrs. Weathers (b.1935) would have been a teenager and also age appropriate to have been in high school when Brushy died in 1950. During this period of time, Mrs. Weathers was a Hamilton, Texas resident where Brushy and his wife resided until moving to Hico (a few miles away) in August of 1949.

Remember, Brushy declared never telling anyone he was Billy the Kid prior to the Morrison interviews in 1949. Brushy even asserted not informing his wife until his return from his visit with the New Mexico governor in 1950. After reading the narrative from Mrs. Weathers, I think you will agree this represents another considerable discrepancy. It appears Brushy was more than happy to *spin his yarn* on the streets of Hamilton and Hico, Texas to anyone lending an ear. I believe the message expressed by Mrs. Weathers provides additional insight into Brushy's psyche during the latter years of his life.

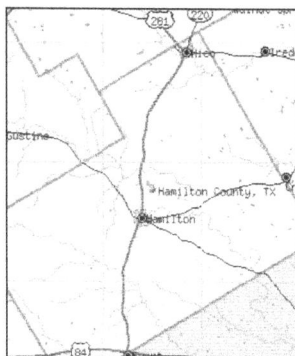

Hamilton County, Texas, showing relative locations of Hamilton, Texas and Hico, Texas. Brushy lived in both at different times. He died in Hico, Texas, and was buried in Hamilton, Texas.

PUTTING IT ALL TOGETHER, A REASONABLE THEORY

I now propose an overall theory regarding Brushy Bill Roberts' claim as Billy the Kid. Brushy (Oliver Pleasant Roberts), well known within his own family as a storyteller, was fascinated by folklore of the Old West. In the late 1930s and nearing 60 years of age, I believe Brushy was consumed with the psychological desire of becoming a person of great historical importance. I believe at this time, he began constructing his web of deception in an attempt to assume the identity of the legendary Billy the Kid.

Between the 1930 and 1940 censuses, Brushy magically increased his age from 52 to 70 by changing his actual date of birth of August 26, 1879 to December 31, 1868. I believe this change was likely for purposes of falsely qualifying as over 65 years of age in the newly introduced social security program. Later, however, while planning his story construction, Brushy realized he required additional age to support his Billy the Kid claim.

I believe by personal acquaintance or published obituary, Brushy discovered the death of William S. Roberts (b.1858, d.1936). Although Brushy and William S. possessed the same last name, there was no family relationship. William S. Roberts' father was James Henry Roberts (b.1839 d.1893) and his grandfather was Benjamin Roberts (b.1800 d.1859). The James Henry Roberts family migrated from Mississippi, settling in San Augustine, Texas in 1871. San Augustine is a town 35 miles east of Nacogdoches, Texas. Early in the Morrison interviews, Brushy stated Nacogdoches, Texas as the location his mythical grandfather, Benjamin Roberts, and family settled.

I believe Brushy realized the birth year of William S. Roberts (b.1858) was appropriate for Billy the Kid. He recognized a birth year in the proximity of 1858 - 1860 was necessary to align with historical accounts of Billy the Kid's age. For Brushy's imaginary family construction, he required a father and a grandfather, so he incorporated the names of William S.' father (James Henry

Roberts) and grandfather (Benjamin Roberts) within his fable. By creatively using names and dates involving this family, Brushy could magically create his ancestry and become the proper age of the legendary Billy the Kid. By the time of the Morrison interviews, Brushy changed his year of birth to 1859, although keeping the December 31 portion of his previously fabricated date of birth. Using December 31, 1859, he would now have been 21 years of age the night of July 14, 1881 when Billy allegedly met his demise, fitting nicely with historical accounts.

Now at last ... Brushy had invented his Roberts family complete with a father, James Henry Roberts; a grandfather, Benjamin Roberts; and a solution for his age difficulty. Furthermore, Brushy created a birth year for his imaginary father, James Henry Roberts. Since Brushy's newly created birth year was twenty years earlier than his actual birth year of 1879, it seemed logical for his faux father to be twenty years older than his actual father, Henry Oliver Roberts. Since Henry Oliver was born in 1852, is it any surprise Brushy stated his fantasy father, James Henry Roberts, was born in 1832?

In the book *The Authentic Life of Billy the Kid* by Pat Garrett (readily available during Brushy's lifetime and now available from Sunstone Press in their Southwest Heritage Series), the date of birth for Henry McCarty, aka Billy the Kid, was stated as November 23, 1859. Although historians doubt the accuracy of that date, it is conveniently similar to Brushy's created birthdate of December 31, 1859. Brushy desired to sound even more imaginative by stating his time of birth as the last hour of the last day of 1859. This colorful Brushy confabulation is practically poetic, don't you agree?

By claiming to assume the identity of dead cousin Ollie (actually Brushy's true identity), Brushy would have an excuse for his continued use of the names Ollie Roberts, Ollie P. Roberts, Oliver Roberts, Oliver Pleasant Roberts, and O. P. Roberts within public documents throughout life. With Brushy's assumption of his own identity, a magical aging of 20 years, and the creative construction of a fictitious Roberts family genealogy, Brushy's yarn could become more believable. Over the years it has certainly fooled a number of authors, researchers, and Brushy believers.

I propose Brushy (Oliver Pleasant Roberts) became immensely fascinated with Billy the Kid stories and folklore during his lifetime. He likely read books and articles available and over time, became reasonably well versed with historical characters, events, and dates. A number of Brushy's departures from historical accounts can be attributed to variations and discrepancies among authors and historians. In addition, many have maintained the long-existing belief Pat Garrett did not kill Billy the Kid. Brushy's fantasy, aided and substantially enhanced by several authors, was even deemed credible enough for inclusion in the introductory portion of the movie, *Young Guns II*, as well as a number of documentaries and nationally televised programs including *Unsolved Mysteries*.

Many have crowned Brushy as the true Billy the Kid due to details of events and participants he described leading up to and during the Lincoln County War. My contrary view is anyone with average intelligence could become well versed with names, dates, and events by studying a topic diligently over a number of years, likely with considerably more accuracy than Brushy exhibited.

Often overlooked by many, Brushy's narrative was aided by details written in notebooks. At the time the Morrison interviews began in June 1949, a number of notebooks existed containing Brushy's writings. Within these reported notebooks, Brushy cleverly outlined his amazing fantasy, complete with names, dates, and events. Many have marveled over the details (many of them inaccurate) Brushy recalled in his interviews. Individuals fail to realize he was not speaking entirely from constructed memory regarding his complex fable. Morrison stated, "These were a series of paper covered composition books and a couple of loose-leaf notebooks in which he had written up his history the way he wanted it told." I consider this quote by Morrison incredibly revealing.

Brushy's notebooks were never examined thoroughly. Morrison suggested Brushy burned or destroyed three pertinent ones prior to his November 1950 press event with the New Mexico governor, Thomas J. Mabry. This well-documented *publicity event* proclaiming Brushy as Billy the Kid was under the guise of seeking a pardon for Billy the Kid's murder conviction of

Sheriff William Brady. This pardon was promised by Governor Lew Wallace to Billy the Kid many years earlier. In the book, *Alias Billy the Kid* (Sonnichsen, Morrison, 1955), we have this explanation:

There is a possibility that he did write down some of the things he was trying to hide. Three of his notebooks have disappeared. Morrison had a brief look at them, but the old man would not allow him to make a real examination or to take many notes. After his death, Morrison and Mrs. Roberts looked for those books and could not find them. Morrison thinks Brushy destroyed them just before he left for his disastrous interview with the governor in Santa Fe.

In summary, within his notebooks, Brushy enhanced his deception by creating variations in events not well documented. Aided by discrepancies existing among historians and authors, he inserted himself into pseudo-history as Billy the Kid. Who knows? Perhaps Brushy even believed his own narrative during the latter years of his life. From the time Brushy's story construction began, he had ample time to creatively accomplish his extreme age increase of twenty years, create a fictional genealogy, and create the dead cousin Ollie yarn as an excuse for using his true name throughout his life. In addition, prior to his first interview with Morrison in 1949, he had ample opportunity to fill his notebooks with creative details regarding historically unknown and/or disputed events. Brushy's imagination and creativity all came together with the publication of his fantasy, titled *Alias Billy the Kid* (Sonnichsen, Morrison, 1955). Over the years, Brushy believer authors have further enhanced Brushy's confabulations with additional false genealogical creations, historical account modifications, and the use of incredibly weak witness statements consisting of hearsay, third party, and rumor testimonials.

Of course, it is likely hardcore Brushy believers will continue to hold on to their belief Brushy was Billy the Kid. Even when confronted with a preponderance of evidence, reality is often ignored when one's mind has been convinced otherwise. For those with an open mind, I have more for your consideration. The following chapter details many of Brushy's timeline conflicts, both within his own story and departures from historical accounts. Please read on.

Pencil sketch of Brushy with William V. Morrison.
Sketch courtesy of Linda Weatherman.

Brushy identified the woman in this picture as his half aunt, Catherine Ann Bonney
(McCarty, Antrim). Although Catherine McCarty Antrim is generally acknowledged as
the actual mother of Henry McCarty, aka Billy the Kid, the legitimacy of this image
as Catherine is disputed. Image from the Rose Collection, #2170, Western History
Collections, University of Oklahoma Libraries.

My mother, Eulaine Haws, at the gravesite of Catherine McCarty Antrim (mother of Henry McCarty, aka Billy the Kid), Memory Lane Cemetery, Silver City, New Mexico.

Brushy's Timeline Conflicts

As mentioned earlier, Brushy imparted his life experiences to Morrison based on claimed memories and accounts detailed throughout his notebooks. To the contrary, I found many timeline conflicts differing from historical accounts of events, in addition to Brushy's superposition in two or more places at the same time. Some clashes are relatively minor, while others are exceedingly incompatible, impossible to explain. In this chapter, I discuss a number of his more troubling timeline pitfalls.

1. Brushy alleged his half aunt, Catherine Ann Bonney, assumed his custody in 1862 after the death of his fantasy mother, Mary Adeline Dunn Roberts. Brushy stated Catherine traveled from the Indian Territory to recover him, relocating for a short time in Colorado, and finally settling in Silver City, New Mexico. Brushy declared remaining in Silver City until he was 12 years of age, then departing Silver City in 1872 to live two years with his fictional father, James Henry Roberts. History indicates, however, Catherine and young Henry McCarty (whose name Brushy claimed as his alias) had not yet arrived in Silver City, New Mexico until 1873 with Henry remaining in Silver City until 1875.

Most historical accounts agree Catherine McCarty Antrim was the mother of Henry McCarty, aka Billy the Kid. Based on research of census records, Catherine's other son, Joseph, was born in New York in 1863. Catherine resided in Indiana from about 1865 until 1869. After marrying William Henry Harrison Antrim, Catherine, with young Henry and Joseph, arrived in Silver City, New Mexico in 1873. After his arrest and escape from jail over a theft incident, Henry departed Silver City late September 1875. From Brushy's narrative, he left Silver City, New Mexico in 1872 to live with his make-believe father in Texas until 1874. This time conflict is rather difficult to explain.

Brushy's conflicts in time, details, and locations are extensive. Granted, although minor variances exist in researcher accounts, how could Brushy have it so wrong? Mixing fact with fiction often results in narrative not properly withstanding the *smell test*. In Brushy's case, his stated timeline represented not only a substantial departure from historical fact, but would require his existence in two places at the same time. Next, I will relate additional Brushy timeline divergence difficulties during this same period.

2. Brushy professed returning to Carlton, Texas in late 1872 and residing for two years with his imaginary father, James Henry Roberts. Brushy alleged staying until May 1874, leaving to join a cattle drive through the Indian Territory. In the Morrison interviews, however, Brushy stated his alleged half aunt, Catherine Bonney McCarty, raised him from the age of under three to twelve. Catherine married William H. Antrim in Santa Fe, New Mexico, relocating the family to Silver City, New Mexico. This well-documented marriage occurred March 1, 1873. We know the real Henry McCarty, aka Billy the Kid, attended the wedding and is shown as a documented witness on the marriage certificate. Maybe Brushy made the trip from his mythical father's home to attend the wedding in Santa Fe, New Mexico, then returned to his father's home. Perhaps the marriage event was not worthy of mentioning during the interviews. It's possible, right? But historical records show Henry McCarty, aka Billy the Kid, was in Silver City until September of 1875 when arrested for a theft. Brushy, however, avowed leaving his non-existent father's Carlton, Texas residence in May 1874 to join a cattle drive, beginning years of various fanciful adventures. Can you reconcile the discrepancy with a reasonable explanation? I certainly can't.

More of this time conflict is illustrated from Henry McCarty's childhood friends (Louis Abraham, Harry Whitehill, and Charley Stevens), placing Henry McCarty in school in Silver City, New Mexico in January of 1874. At that time, Henry McCarty was residing with his mother, Catherine (Brushy claimed as his half aunt), during the last nine months of her life. Catherine died September 16, 1874. I repeat again, Brushy contended to be in Carlton, Texas from late 1872 until May 1874 before heading out on a cattle drive, beginning several years of imaginative escapades. Could Brushy have been in two different places at the same time again? It appears Brushy believers and hoaxers think so. Of course, the obvious and proper explanation for this time conflict is entirely due to Brushy's complete story fabrication. It was still years yet before his birth as Oliver Pleasant Roberts in August 1879.

3. Brushy declared while in the Indian Territory in 1874 (prior to Oklahoma statehood in 1890), he left a cattle drive to become employed by Belle Reed (later known as Belle Starr). Brushy described his three-month employment at her ranch near Briartown (now in Oklahoma). At that time, however, Belle Reed was living in Scyene, Texas (Dallas County). Belle's first husband, Jim Reed, was killed August 6, 1874 near Paris, Texas. It was not until 1880, when Belle married a Cherokee man, Sam Starr, that she relocated to the Indian Territory and began her criminal endeavors. Yet, Brushy declared leaving her employment in the Indian Territory in August or September of 1874. The truth of this episode would require Belle present in two places at the same time. Young Henry McCarty, aka Billy the Kid, was still in Silver City, New Mexico during this time. This portion of Brushy's creativity would actually require both Belle and Brushy in two different places simultaneously.

Belle Star, 1848–1889, notorious Old West outlaw. Brushy claimed employment by Belle for three months in the Indian Territory while she was still living in Texas.

One bothersome note regarding Brushy's episode with Belle is his colorful description of the James and Younger outlaws bringing sacks of stolen money to Belle for splitting. Brushy recounted Belle as saying, "This is your part and this is my part." Although it is true Belle was acquainted with the James and Younger Gang members, I have considerable doubt they would split their ill-gotten gains with anyone other than themselves. Of course, this fascinating event never happened since in 1874 Belle was residing in Texas and five years remained before Brushy (Oliver Pleasant Roberts) would be born.

4. Historical records show Henry McCarty, aka Billy the Kid, arrested September 23, 1875 in Silver City, New Mexico for stealing clothes from a Chinese laundry. Henry promptly escaped from jail and fled Silver City, New Mexico. On February 17, 1877 in Globe, Arizona, he was arrested again and taken to Cedar Springs, Arizona where he promptly escaped. Then March 25, 1877, Henry was once again arrested and managed to escape from a Fort Grant, Arizona guardhouse.

Brushy reported returning to Silver City, New Mexico upon the death of his alleged half aunt, Catherine, September 16, 1874. Shortly after Catherine's funeral, he described departing with his friend Mountain Bill on an escapade lasting several years. They allegedly gallivanted throughout Montana, Oregon, Wyoming, and Nebraska with Brushy entering various horse riding events.

How can the publicly documented arrests of Henry McCarty, aka Billy the Kid, reconcile with Brushy's account? They can't. Brushy did not claim to be in any of the aforementioned arrest locations at the designated times. He only described traveling in Montana, Oregon, Wyoming, and Nebraska entering horse riding events with his fabricated friend, Mountain Bill. This discrepancy represents an impossible timeline conflict. Of course, Brushy (Oliver Pleasant Roberts) was certainly not arrested in those locations nor was he entering horse riding events. It would still be years before his birth in August 1879 in Arkansas. Do you see how effortless this time and location difficulty was to resolve?

5. Brushy asserted riding to Mesilla, New Mexico during the summer of 1877. Brushy maintained that together with Tom O'Keefe, he then departed Mesilla for Loving's Bend near Phoenix, New Mexico (a town that began its existence in 1889, just south of present day Carlsbad, New Mexico). It is historically recorded Henry McCarty, aka Billy the Kid, committed his first murder by killing Frank P. Cahill August 17, 1877 at Camp Grant, Arizona (near Tucson). I suppose this tight window of time does not completely disprove Brushy's account since summer does consist of several months. It is remotely possible for these two events not to conflict. What is actually more bothersome is why Brushy would fail to mention the first man killed by Billy the Kid, especially when discussing the summer of 1877? Wouldn't that rather substantial detail be worthy of mentioning?

6. From historical accounts, John Tunstall was killed by Sheriff Brady's posse late afternoon, Monday, February 18, 1878. On Wednesday morning, February 20, Billy the Kid and Fred Waite were taken prisoner by Sheriff Brady. Billy and Fred were not released from jail until Saturday, February 23, 1878. John Tunstall's funeral was held Thursday, February 21, 1878. Historical accounts show Billy the Kid was not at John Tunstall's funeral, due to his incarceration at the time.

Yet, from the interviews with Morrison, Brushy stated, "None of the Murphy boys were present at the funeral of Tunstall when we buried his body behind the Tunstall store."

Historical accounts indicate Billy was upset over his inability to attend Tunstall's funeral. Brushy, however, maintained attending the funeral and burial during the time Billy was still incarcerated. This would have required his presence at two different places simultaneously. Of course, Brushy was not there at all since it's still more than a year before he (Oliver Pleasant Roberts) would exit his mother's womb.

7. Brushy stated in his Morrison interviews, "Selman fought on our side in that cattle business in 1878."

In 1877, the famous lawman turned outlaw, John Selman, and family moved to Fort Griffin, Shackelford County, Texas. Selman assumed a position as the Deputy Inspector for Hides. History records Selman as a hunted man by vigilantes after his partner was killed June 24, 1878 over a hide theft incident. Later in 1879, he established residence in Lincoln County, New Mexico.

The Lincoln County War was generally considered over at the conclusion of the five-day Battle of Lincoln, July 19, 1878. John Selman is not mentioned in historical accounts as a participant in this battle or any earlier event during the Lincoln County War.

Although John Selman later created substantial havoc with his criminal activity in Lincoln County, it is clear he was not a participant in the Lincoln County War of 1878. It appears Brushy showed the remarkable consistency of including as many famous names as possible throughout his yarns, with little regard for historical accuracy.

John Selman, 1839–1896, lawman who later turned outlaw shortly after the Lincoln County War. Photograph from the Rose Collection, #2137, Western History Collections, University of Oklahoma Libraries.

8. A newspaper article regarding Brushy titled "Texan Knew Bad Men, Saw Hoss Thieves Hang" written by Mr. Thomas Turner, was published in the September 18, 1950 issue of the *Dallas Morning News*. This article included a quote from Brushy regarding his mythical father, James Henry Roberts. Brushy's quote reads as follows: "He was a scout with Kit Carson … him and Carson tried to warn Custer he couldn't lick them five tribes of Indians, but he wouldn't listen. So they took out. And they were right."

Most historical accounts involving Custer report six Indian tribes, but let's not *sweat* the small stuff. The primary problem is Kit Carson died May 23, 1868 while the Battle of Little Big Horn occurred more than eight years later during June 23-26, 1876. I suppose the only logical explanation for this untruth must be that Brushy's imaginary father, James Henry Roberts, lied to him. Of course, in reality, Brushy just didn't do enough homework for this portion of his pseudo-history to have any semblance of believability.

George Armstrong Custer, 1839–1876.

9. Brushy described his employments during the years of 1888 through 1893. During this five year period, he professed employments as a field leader for the Anti-Horse Thief Association, as a Deputy Marshall for U.S. Marshal Force, as a detective with the Pinkerton detectives arresting train robbers, as an officer for the famous Judge Parker of Fort Smith, Arkansas, and as a bronc rider in bucking horse events in Wyoming, Oregon, and Old Mexico. Brushy's list of employments is incredibly long and I'm not through just yet. In addition, during this same five year interval, he asserted training to become a professional boxer and traveling to Argentina on a horse breaking expedition. I suppose one could stretch their imagination enough to believe all these employments occurred in such a short period of time. Let's take a look and examine the feasibility of these claims.

With Brushy's many employments from 1888 through 1893, one job alone required four years. In the fall of 1888, Brushy purported joining the Anti-Horse Thief Association for purposes of clearing out Texas horse thieves. He described riding up and down the Red River in East Texas and Indian Territory. In the Morrison interviews, Brushy stated:

Judge Parker, a United States judge at Fort Smith Arkansas, asked me to go into the Ozark Mountains to pick up the many gangs of thieves operating there. ... It took us four years to break them up.

Brushy offered imaginative details for this experience, but the key consideration is the four years relegated to accomplish this one task. This four year consumption of time allowed only one year remaining in the five year period to complete his many other stated employments. This is beginning to represent a rather considerable timeline difficulty.

A side note: It seems unlikely Billy the Kid would take such a huge risk associating with Hanging Judge Parker and lawmen he would most certainly encounter. Does this appear to be a risk Billy the Kid would take? Of course, Brushy had an explanation. In the Morrison interviews, he stated:

Judge Parker of Fort Smith, Arkansas told me he knew who I was when I came up for appointment as Deputy United States Marshal, and at first said he would not have any outlaws working for him. However, he changed his mind.

It appears Brushy expected us to believe the famous Hanging Judge Parker would knowingly have Billy the Kid working for him.

Judge Isaac Parker, 1838-1896.
He was know as the "Hanging Judge" of the American Old West.

This Brushy statement appears logically unsatisfying. I believe if Hanging Judge Parker knew Billy the Kid was in his presence, he would have been immediately taken into custody and either returned to New Mexico by law enforcement or Judge Parker would have carried out the penalty for Billy's murder conviction at the end of a rope. After all, Hanging Judge Parker had quite a historical reputation to uphold.

Now, let's revisit the five-year timeline with four years already exhausted. Not including considerable travel time, six months of the remaining year involved Brushy's trip to Argentina (Argentine Republic). From the Morrison interviews, Brushy said, "In 1893, my riding skill gave me a trip to the Argentine Republic. We left Oklahoma City about the tenth of January 1893 and sailed to Buenos Aires. After we were there some six months, they suggested that we have a contest ride."

Brushy described his remarkable horse breaking experiences in Argentina, clearly stating he was there for six months. After considerable travel time to South America and back, only a few months would remain to accomplish his other employments in the five-year period from 1888 through 1893. Only a short time would remain for employment with the Pinkerton Agency catching train robbers, training as a professional boxer, becoming a Deputy with the U.S. Marshall Service, and participating in bucking horse events in Wyoming, Oregon, and Mexico. It's quite a stretch to one's imagination, isn't it? It would not be a surprise if some Brushy believers rectify such impossibilities by suggesting some kind of Brushy clone involvement.

10. In the September 18, 1950 issue of the *Dallas Morning News*, a Thomas Turner article quoted Brushy as stating: "In 1885 I joined Buffalo Bill's show at Pueblo, Colorado for about a year. Then I went with Pawnee Bill's show ... I come back to Texas and organized my own show. For twenty-five years toured all over the Southwest with it."

There are many difficulties with this Brushy quote. First, in this interview and all others I have found from articles and book accounts, never once has Brushy stated the name of his Wild West show. If one had a Wild West show operating for twenty-five years, wouldn't there be a name of it somewhere in newspapers or magazines? Nothing in regard to a name for this show has been found in any published account. All we have is Brushy's word he operated such a show for twenty-five years.

The real difficulty pertains to the number of time conflicts this statement represents. Brushy professed joining the Buffalo Bill Wild West Show in 1885, remaining for a year, and later participating in Pawnee Bill's show. Pawnee Bill's Wild West Show began in 1888. Assuming Brushy was onboard at the opening with Pawnee Bill and remained as little as a year, it would imply Brushy opened his own show no earlier than 1889. Since Brushy stated operating his show for twenty-five years, this would entail Brushy touring the Southwest from 1889 through 1914. This directly conflicts with events and locations described earlier involving his many (too many) employments from 1888 through 1893. Additional discrepancies contradicting his twenty-five year operation of a Wild West show include ranching in Mexico with two partners from 1907 through 1914, fighting with Pancho Villa in Mexico in 1910, and marrying twice and divorcing once in Van Zandt County, Texas from 1909 through 1912. Other time conflicts exist, but I believe I have provided enough. Do you see the problems with Brushy's quote in the 1950 *Dallas Morning News* article? Do Brushy believers have an explanation for these numerous conflicts? I'm quite certain they do, but we should remember at the time of his alleged employment with Buffalo Bill in 1885, Brushy (Oliver Pleasant Roberts) was a six year old child in the care of his parents.

Buffalo Bill Cody, 1846–1917. He performed in Wild West shows from 1883–1906.

11. In the fall of 1894, Brushy alleged rejoining the U.S. Marshal Force serving three more years. Yet, in 1895, he professed leaving from El Paso, Texas with cowboy friends to raise livestock in Mexico. Brushy described ranching through the years of 1896 and 1897. Wouldn't it be difficult to be employed by the U.S. Marshall Service from 1894 through 1897 while ranching in Mexico from 1896 through 1897? This time Brushy has successfully managed the feat of two employments in different countries simultaneously. Of course, in reality, Brushy (Oliver Pleasant Roberts) was still in his teens and living with his parents in Sulphur Springs, Texas.

12. During the spring of 1898, Brushy contended enlisting in Muskogee, Oklahoma as one of Roosevelt's Rough Riders for participation in the Spanish American War. Allegedly, he was transferred to San Antonio, Texas, went through Mobile, Alabama, and not long before he landed in Cuba. While this might not represent an absolute hole in Brushy's yarn, I question the not long part. The actual Rough Riders departed May 27, 1898 and arrived in Cuba on June 22, 1898. I suppose not long could actually be just under a month, if very patient.

Brushy provided some detail of his experience including an interesting caveat involving an officer. Within this episode, Brushy referenced a Lieutenant Cook recognizing him. After examining military records of the Rough Riders, I found no Lieutenant Cook on this expedition.

During a two-month portion of his avouched time in Cuba, Brushy purported that while riding with a scout gang hunting the enemy, he saw "scouts shot on every side of him." The two-month duration represents a time difficulty with Brushy's account. The Rough Riders arrived in Cuba June 22, 1898. The fighting was mostly over after the Battle of San Juan Hill July 1, 1898. On July 17, the Spanish forces in Santiago surrendered to General Shafter of the United States military. On August 14, the Rough Riders arrived back in the United States at Long Island, New York. The time of arrival of the Rough Riders in Cuba to the time of their return in New York was less than two months. Yet, Brushy reported riding with a scout gang for two months. How does one reconcile this discrepancy? Maybe Brushy stayed behind in Cuba for some reason, not returning with the Rough Riders; or perhaps, he just misstated the length of time he was there.

A side note: Historical records show the cavalry was mostly dismounted and operated as infantry. Only a portion of the horses arrived in Cuba with the troops. The horses making the trip were primarily assigned to officers. As a new enlistee, Brushy certainly would not have been an officer. Yet, Brushy attested training enlistees to ride horses. Of course, by now we have become accustomed to Brushy's confabulations flying in the face of historical accounts, haven't we?

Another rather perplexing statement was made by Brushy during the Morrison interviews: "During a battle one day, there were four officers shot in the back. They thought the Cherokee Indian and I did it, which they tried to prove in a court martial, but failed. When our time was out, they gave us a bobtailed discharge."

One would think military records would exist detailing four officers shot in the back and the subsequent court martial. Events of the Spanish American War appear to be well documented, yet no records indicate any such occurrence. I suppose we are to believe these murders too insignificant for documentation in military records. Do you believe that?

The discrepancies within Brushy's account of this wondrous adventure are seemingly difficult to explain. I do, however, have an explanation. The solution to this dilemma is simple. Brushy (Oliver Pleasant Roberts) wasn't there. At the time of the Spanish American War, Brushy was still residing with his parents in Sulphur Springs, Texas.

13. Brushy reported establishing a ranch known as Three Bar in Mexico with two partners in 1907. As the Mexican revolution began in 1910, Brushy purportedly fought under Pancho Villa and was selected as Captain of 106 men. This is perhaps a bit difficult to believe, but let's continue with this fable as it further unravels. Ultimately in 1914, Brushy claimed his two partners and him left Mexico losing all their assets valued at $200,000. That's truly a substantial amount of money for that time. $200,000 in 1914 would be equivalent to nearly five million dollars today. Well, for the moment, let's pretend this unlikely claim possible too.

Now, let's examine the time conflict. Brushy married a lady named Anna Lee July 11, 1909 in Texas, divorced her November 10, 1910 in Texas, and showed up on the census in 1910 as residing in Van Zandt County, Texas. Anna was the first of Brushy's four wives during his lifetime. Although Brushy failed to mention Anna in his interviews with Morrison, he did disclose his other three wives. Brushy married his second wife Mollie Brown August 21, 1912 in Van Zandt County, Texas. Brushy successfully managed marrying twice, divorcing once, and residing in Van Zandt County, Texas during the same period he was operating an incredibly successful ranch in Mexico from 1907 through 1914. Examining a map, you will find Van Zandt County quite a distance from the Mexican border (more than 450 miles). I believe frequent commutes via horseback or an early automobile unrealistic, wouldn't you?

14. Brushy married Mollie Brown in 1912; she died in 1919. For purposes of this time conflict, let's disregard Brushy's claim of residing in Mexico from 1907 through 1914. Brushy specified his employments during the time interval while married to Mollie. These included a trading business in Oklahoma; riding bucking horses (with Brushy's claimed birth date, he would have already been 53 years of age in 1912 when he married Mollie, quite an advanced age to be riding bucking horses); working in the oil fields of Oklahoma; and as a plain-clothesman officer in Gladewater after oil was struck in East Texas. It is interesting to note the first Gladewater, Texas oil well blew in April 7, 1931. Perhaps Brushy wasn't specifically referring to Gladewater for his officer employment during the East Texas oil boom. It is clear, however, there was no oil boom anywhere in East Texas until about 1930. Yet, Brushy described this employment prior to Mollie's death in 1919 was due to the East Texas oil boom not yet in existence. How does this logic compute? I'm fairly certain the Brushy believers will contend that even though Brushy was describing the time period when he was married to Mollie Brown, he just was fuzzy regarding when the oil boom in East Texas occurred. There's always a believer explanation, right?

15. The following issue is debatable and subject to interpretation. At times, Morrision would ask questions not readily answered by Brushy. It's conjecture, but I suspect Brushy's notes were no help in allowing providing credible responses to unanticipated questions. Brushy commented to Morrison in regard to the difficulty of bringing details of far-off events of his life into focus: "Sixty-nine years is a long time to recollect some of those things."

Morrision's interviews with Brushy began in June of 1949, continuing over the course of a year. It is not known the exact date of this portion of the interviews, but based on Brushy's story progression, I believe it was in 1949. I find it interesting the actual age of Oliver Pleasant Roberts in 1949 would have been 69 until his birthday on August 26. Is this a coincidence? Brushy believers will happily discount this as a coincidence since 1879-1880 represents a time when the Lincoln County War had recently ended with Billy the Kid a hunted man. I personally believe it a slip of Brushy's tongue yielding his true age (69), rather than his fabricated age (89). However, I'll leave the choice of interpretation with the reader.

Twenty-four More Holes in Brushy's Fable

During the interviews with Morrison, Brushy conveyed his account of events and occurrences before, during, and after the Lincoln County War. Brushy's recollections often departed significantly from historical accounts. Although differing versions of events exist among historians, many of Brushy's accounts represent obvious departures from fact. In other statements by Brushy, conflicts and falsehoods either exist within his accounts or are just difficult to believe. Among his many discrepancies and stretches of imagination, I believe the following are significantly worthy of mention:

1. An interview with Brushy was published in the September 18, 1950 issue of the Dallas Morning News. The article was titled "Texan Knew Bad Men, Saw Hoss Thieves Hang" written by Thomas Turner, consisting of statements by Brushy a few months before his death in December 1950. One interesting quote pertained to his supposed first meeting with the famous outlaw, Jesse James. Per Brushy, "first time I ever seen him I was about ten. He come to our house, wounded. Had a bullet hole in his shoulder you could see daylight through. I watched my mother wrap a rag 'round a stick, put something on it and swab out the hole."

Jesse James, 1847–1882.
Jesse James died when Brushy was two years old.

Brushy elaborated more regarding this experience in a taped interview September 6, 1949 with Morrey Davidson. The resulting program was titled *The True Jesse James Story*. In regard to his first encounter with Jesse James, Brushy stated:

He come to my mother's house when I was about seven years old, with his arm just about shot off. He stayed there six weeks. My mother doctored his arm 'til it got better and Frank take him away from there too.

Well, which is it, ten years or seven years of age? Brushy exhibited some inconsistency, but let's not make this an issue. Brushy alleged as a child of about ten (or seven) years of age, he met Jesse James when his mother treated Jesse's wound. Since Brushy asserted to have been born in 1859, this occurrence would supposedly have been about 1869 (or 1866). During that time period, consistent with his own story, Brushy would have still been in Trinidad, Colorado in the care of his professed half aunt (not mother), Catherine Bonney (McCarty, Antrim). I suppose he could have considered his half aunt as mother (Brushy asserted she raised him from the age of three), so I won't make an issue out of that portion of his fantasy. However, during the time period of 1866 through 1869 or any other time, what connection existed between Catherine and Jesse James to have afforded her the opportunity to treat the wounds of the famous outlaw? Brushy provided no explanation for this difficulty.

The actual unexplainable problem, however, pertains to Jesse's location from 1866 through 1869. During this time frame, Jesse James was busy robbing banks in Missouri, Iowa, West Virginia, and Texas with no reports of incidents resulting in his wounding. There appears to be no recognized historical accounts of Jesse visiting Colorado (or even other locations where Catherine had resided), allowing Jesse the opportunity of meeting young Henry McCarty, later to be known as Billy the Kid. This hogwash was indeed colorful, yet this fallacy is easily explained. It would be another seven years after 1869 before Brushy's parents, Henry Oliver Roberts and Sara Elizabeth Ferguson, would marry and begin their family.

2. Discrepancies between historical accounts of events during the Lincoln County War and Brushy's alleged recollections include the following:

a. Historical accounts reflect a five-day battle in 1878, known as The Battle of Lincoln. Brushy described it as a three-day battle.
b. In an incident involving crawling over an adobe wall after Sheriff Brady

and his deputies were ambushed, Brushy claimed Fred Waite joined him. Historical accounts indicate it was Jim French, not Fred Waite, who climbed over the adobe wall with Billy. According to Brushy, Fred Waite was wounded in the incident, while it was actually Jim French.

c. In an additional incident during the Lincoln County War, Brushy stated his faction captured Billy Morton and Frank Baker. Brushy asserted he killed both men during an escape attempt. Historical accounts do not credit these killings specifically to Billy the Kid.

d. During the infamous escape from the Lincoln County courthouse, Billy the Kid killed Deputies J. W. Bell and Robert Olinger. In the Morrison interviews, Brushy stated, "At noontime as usual, Olinger went across the street with other prisoners for lunch." Most historical accounts indicate the time of day as between 5 and 6 PM, not noon.

e. Brushy professed trading his tintype image to an Indian lady (Deluvina Maxwell) in exchange for a scarf. The chain of custody of the tintype image has been clearly established and does not include Deluvina. I will delve into more detail regarding the tintype image possession in a later discussion.

Perhaps these are only minor detail discrepancies and nothing of great significance. I point out these differences since these disparities agree exactly with those given in a book published in 1925 titled *The Saga of Billy the Kid* by Walter Noble Burns. This book was readily available to the general public during the time period when I believe Brushy was crafting his fable. Are Brushy's historical errors just unfortunate coincidences with the identical errors stated by Mr. Burns?

3. Although not necessarily a hole in Brushy's myth, I believe it appropriate to discuss a detail he mentioned which some authors believe lends credence to his knowledge of previously unknown facts.

In the prologue of the book, *Alias Billy the Kid* (Sonnichsen, Morrison, 1955), an issue is raised supporting Brushy's knowledge of a specific event few supposedly knew. During the five-day Battle of Lincoln from July 15th-19th, 1878, there was involvement of Colonel Dudley and his troops. Within this prologue, Mr. Sonnichsen stated:

And there were things in Brushy Bill's story that made one

wonder. How did he know that negro soldiers from Fort Stanton took positions on the hillside and joined in the firing that day when the Murphy men burned McSween's house?" Not many people know about that.

For Brushy believers this is strong evidence Brushy was present since not many supposedly knew this detail. It appears, however, Morrison and Sonnichsen fell short in their research. Historical records indicate Nathan Augustus Monroe Dudley was in command of the all-black 9th cavalry. By 1925, literature describing black trooper involvement had already been published. On page 124 of the book, *The Saga of Billy the Kid* by Walter Noble Burns published in 1925, it clearly states some troopers were black. I am not implying black soldiers fired on Billy and others during the Battle of Lincoln encounter. I am only suggesting Brushy likely read this account and included it within his fable. I believe he read and studied this particular book while planning his elaborate narrative. Although historians discount the accuracy of events described in this book, it certainly provides significant detail cited by Brushy regarding the Lincoln County War and circumstances surrounding the supposed demise of Billy the Kid.

4. In his interviews with Morrison, Brushy provided a motive for the April 1, 1878 ambush of Sheriff Brady and his deputies. "Sheriff Brady was gunning for me with warrants for cattle stealing." However, it was late in 1878, after the conclusion of the Lincoln County War in July 1878 when Billy began his cattle rustling activities. Historical accounts reflect the actual motive for the ambush was to prevent Sheriff Brady from killing attorney Alexander McSween, who was returning to Lincoln that day for a court proceeding.

5. Brushy described a December 1880 event at Fort Sumner resulting in the death of his friend, Tom O'Folliard, at Charlie Bowdre's house. Historical accounts credit Pat Garrett's posse with fatally wounding Tom, carrying him inside the Bowdre house where he died.

Morrison's interviews with Brushy were also transcribed by Frederic Bean. Bean's transcriptions of the interviews were published in a 2012 book titled *Billy the Kid ... the Lost Interviews* by W. C. Jameson. In this transcription, Brushy stated:

His cousin, Kip McKinney, Tom's own cousin and one of Garrett's posse, wouldn't give Tom a drink of water when he was a-dying, just let Tom die begging for water, wouldn't give him a drink. I had known McKinney some before all the difficulties and I thought he was a good man. It turned out he was just another coward like the rest of them Murphy men and Garrett men.

A couple of difficulties exist with Brushy's account. First, he stated Kip McKinney as Tom O'Folliard's cousin. Researchers have determined no genealogical connection between Kip McKinney and Tom O'Folliard. Secondly, Kip McKinney denied ever meeting or seeing Billy the Kid prior to the night of July 14, 1881 when Pat Garrett is alleged to have killed Billy.

Of course, there is a good excuse for Brushy's faulty account of this event. In December 1880, Brushy (Oliver Pleasant Roberts) would have been just a year old, in the care of his parents Henry Oliver and Sara Elizabeth Ferguson Roberts.

6. Brushy elaborated regarding Billy's capture late December 1880 by Sheriff Pat Garrett at Stinking Springs, New Mexico. Brushy stated, "As soon as Garrett got elected and with this killing of Carlyle tacked on me, Garrett had an excuse to come after me, which he did." The problem with this pseudo-history motive was that Garrett and his posse were actually seeking Billy the Kid for the murders of Sheriff Brady, Deputy Hindman, and Buckshot Roberts, not Jim Carlyle. I suppose there were so many names of dead people involving Billy the Kid and the Lincoln County War, Brushy obviously confused names and events in his notebooks. At the time this occurred, however, Brushy (Oliver Pleasant Roberts) had just recently celebrated his first birthday in Arkansas.

7. In the Morrison interviews, Brushy contended he could draw and shoot with either hand, yet much quicker and more accurate with his left hand. Brushy bragged while using his left hand, "no one could beat me on the draw."

The only image of Billy the Kid accepted as authentic is the famous tintype image reflecting Billy holding his rifle with his right hand with his revolver on his left. This tintype image was displayed in many publications and articles throughout Brushy's lifetime. However, early photography consisted of what is called a tintype, resulting in a reversed image. The famous tintype of Billy the Kid was subject to this reverse imaging, thus providing only the illusion of a left handed Billy. In reality, Billy was holding the rifle in his left hand with his revolver positioned on his right. Most books, articles, and publications post 1986 have corrected the reverse image by flipping the picture properly illustrating Billy as right handed.

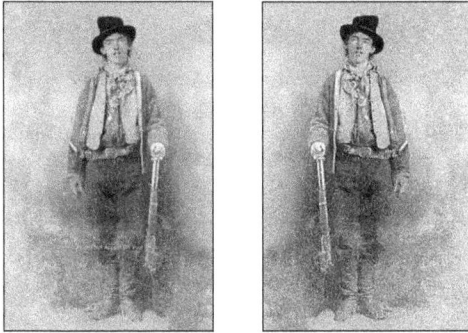

Billy the Kid. The image on the left shows revolver on Billy's right side. The incorrect image is the one on the right.

Could it be Brushy's contention his fast draw with his left hand was due to the tintype reversed image appearing in publications during the time of his fable construction? Many authors, influenced by this tintype image, incorrectly assumed Billy was left handed. After many authors portrayed Billy as left handed, is it really any surprise Brushy would state his quick draw was with his left hand? It certainly doesn't surprise me.

8. Why would Brushy brag of his superb marksmanship, while at other times he could completely miss an easy target?

From historical accounts, on the first of April 1878 in Lincoln, New Mexico, Billy the Kid, with five or more others, ambushed Sheriff William Brady and four deputies. This ambush resulted in the death of Sheriff Brady and Deputy George Hindman.

In this surprise attack, Brushy alleged targeting one specific deputy, Billy Mathews. He professed firing at Mathews in an earlier encounter the day before, but missed. Then in the ambush, aided by the cover of a protective adobe wall and adequate time to aim, Brushy declared missing Mathews again.

Now, let's fast forward in time to the fall of 1888 when Brushy asserted employment with the Anti-Horse Thief Association tasked with clearing Texas of horse thieves. He avouched investigating many cases of counter branding. Brushy was quoted in the Morrison interviews, "Several times, with some quick shooting, I shot the branding iron from the hands of the thief." That's impressive. This sounds much like an Annie Oakley feat or perhaps a stunt from a Lone Ranger movie. It is particularly impressive since one would expect most horse thieves to be well armed. Would someone attempt such a daring shot without knowing if the other person would quickly fire back? Shooting a branding iron out of someone's hands from a distance would require one to have great confidence in their superb marksmanship.

Let's now go back to the original question. How could Brushy have missed hitting Mathews on two occasions, yet claimed such accuracy he shot branding irons out of the hands of thieves? Accounts indicate Mathews was not wounded in the second encounter (there is no reliable account of an earlier encounter). The distance to his target during the ambush was likely less than 50 feet. Brushy's quote to Morrison did not indicate whether he was using his revolver or rifle. It seems likely Billy the Kid would have chosen his Winchester rifle rather than his revolver, thus increasing his advantage in accuracy during the surprise ambush. Still, we are to believe Brushy just missed Mathews with his first shot and subsequent shots in an ambush while specifically targeting him, yet later was so accurate he could exhibit superb feats of marksmanship.

While historical accounts indicate Billy the Kid disliked Billy Mathews, many believe he possessed a much greater hatred for Sheriff Brady. Brady was one of the primary individuals Billy blamed for the death of his friend and employer, John Tunstall. Historical accounts indicate Sheriff Brady was shot nine times in the ambush. I believe Brady was Billy's primary mark with deputies as only secondary targets during the ambush. Most historical accounts indicate Billy as a good to excellent marksman with both a handgun and rifle. In this attack on Brady and his deputies, it would seem highly unlikely, given Billy's talent, to have missed his primary target over the course of the entire ambush. Of course, the easy explanation for Brushy's recollection of this historical event defying logic is easy to explain. Brushy wasn't there. He wasn't even in his mother's womb yet since he (Oliver Pleasant Roberts) was not born until more than a year later in August 1879.

9. Brushy made a peculiarly gigantic mistake while discussing Celsa and Saval Gutierrez. Per Morrison's transcriptions, Brushy said:

> I knew Celsa and Pat's (Pat Garrett's) wife, who were sisters to Saval Gutierrez, before Pat came to this country. Celsa was one of my sweethearts when I was in Fort Sumner. Her brother Saval lived in Fort Sumner. After I returned from hunting Old John, he went up to Canaditas and got Celsa for me. She wanted to go to Mexico with me, but I did not want to get married until Garrett was gone.

Although Brushy's narrative is certainly colorful, it presents an unexplainable enigma. Pat Garrett's wife was Apolinaria Gutierrez. Although Celsa and Apolinaria were sisters, Celsa was Saval Gutierrez's wife, not his sister. How did Brushy have this important detail so wrong? I suspect Brushy read in a book or article Saval was Pat Garrett's brother-in-law, not realizing it was by marriage. Brushy incorrectly assumed the wrong brother-in-law connection by believing Saval, Apolinaria, and Celsa were all siblings. Gutierrez was the maiden name of both Celsa and Apolinaria. Celsa's last name remained the same after the marriage to her cousin, Saval Gutierrez. From his readings, Brushy knew Billy the Kid had girlfriends, but picked the wrong one to claim for this episode. I find it highly unlikely Saval would fetch his wife, Celsa, for a romantic rendezvous with Billy the Kid. Still, Brushy provided us with a nice romantic touch.

Historical recollections portray a romantic relationship of Billy the Kid with Paulita Maxwell, the sister of Pete Maxwell. To my surprise Brushy never once mentioned her name in any portion of the Morrison interviews, yet deemed it necessary to elaborate on a romance that never existed. Brushy

(Oliver Pleasant Roberts) was only one year of age in December 1880 when this event supposedly occurred. Given his memory only consisted from his readings of Billy the Kid, perhaps Brushy took notes from one of the wrong dime store novels.

10. Since Billy the Kid was known for a number of romantic relationships, Brushy obviously felt compelled to weave another love interest into his yarn. Brushy described an unfortunate pick for a sweetheart during 1881. In the Morrison interviews, Brushy proclaimed, "I also stayed at the Yerby Ranch north of Fort Sumner quite a bit. We were good friends. I kept horses and mules there when Charley Bowdre worked for Yerby. He had a good-looking daughter, who was a sort of sweetheart of mine. I don't remember her name."

Yerby's *good-looking* daughter must have made quite an impression with Brushy. So much that even with the help of his notes, he could not recall her name. Let's go ahead and consider this lapse as just the failing memory of a senior citizen. The major problem, however, with Brushy's account pertains to the members of the household of Thomas Yerby. According to the 1880 census for the Yerby family, Thomas had only one daughter, Florentina, shown as two years of age at the time. Perhaps Brushy instead meant thirty year old Thomas Yerby's mistress, eighteen year of age Nasaria. If this had been the case, wouldn't Brushy have known Nasaria was Thomas Yerby's mistress and not his daughter? Oh, I almost forgot ... several dime store distorted accounts of Billy the Kid depicted Nasaria as the daughter of Thomas Yerby. Is it any real surprise how Brushy had it so wrong? It seems Brushy, in his confabulations, again drew from the wrong fanciful account while concocting this portion of his hoax. Of course, in reality, at the time of this romantic episode, Brushy (Oliver Pleasant Roberts) was still an infant under three years of age in the care of his parents.

11. Brushy described participation in a specific bucking horse event during the fall of 1889. He asserted winning a championship at a Cheyenne, Wyoming cowboy roundup by successfully riding the famous horse, Cyclone. Brushy said his friend Tom Waggoner covered all bets and awarded Brushy $10,000 for his spectacular win. Although this huge amount of winnings was remotely possible since gambling was involved, $10,000 was an incredible amount of money in 1889. $10,000 in 1889 would roughly interpolate as equivalent to quarter of a million dollars today. That's quite a prize for the time, isn't it?

In response to Brushy stating no one had successfully ridden Cyclone, I thought perhaps a legendary bucking horse by that name existed in history. My research revealed a famous horse known as Cyclone, with a reputation of throwing 125 riders over a period of seven years. 25 year old Tom Three Persons managed a successful ride in 1912. I speculate Brushy heard or read of this accomplishment, considering his keen interest in horse riding events. Could this explain Brushy's name selection of Cyclone as a nearly impossible to ride horse? The prize awarded to Tom Three Persons was $1000, considered a large cash prize in 1912, yet pales in comparison to the $10,000 in Brushy's fable.

Although it is speculative where Brushy found the name Cyclone, throughout Brushy's tale to Morrison he name-dropped a long list of individuals he imagined to have known. It seems to follow he might well have included the name of a famous horse too. Of course, since Brushy (Oliver Pleasant Roberts) was only 10 years of age in 1889, this episode is obviously just more pure fiction. I'm not really surprised, are you?

12. I happened upon another interesting Brushy horse tale discussed in his interview with Morrison. Brushy described riding for Buffalo Bill Cody in about 1886 at his newly established ranch in North Platte, Nebraska. Of note, Brushy also claimed employment as a scout in the Black Hills of the Dakotas during this same time period. In spite of Brushy's alleged simultaneous employments, I'll continue with this horse story.

Brushy recounted successfully riding a mare named Black Diamond in the open prairie, a performance no one had previously accomplished. Unsurprisingly I found no reports of a horse of that name involving Buffalo Bill on his ranch or in his shows. However, it's quite possible a horse with the name of Black Diamond owned by Buffalo Bill could have existed.

On the other hand, I have a theory as to where Brushy may have derived the horse name of Black Diamond. A famous movie actor of the 1940s, known as Lash LaRue, was featured in popular westerns at the time. The releases of these westerns were before Brushy's interviews with Morrison in 1949. I found it fascinating Lash's horse was Black Diamond. Could Brushy have derived the horse name Black Diamond from Lash LaRue movies or is this just another case of legendary coincidence?

There is certainly one more item of interest regarding Lash LaRue. In 1949, he starred in a movie titled *Son of Billy the Kid* with a plot theorizing Billy the Kid was not killed by Pat Garrett, but lived on to become a respectable citizen. Although for a number of years, Brushy had professed he was Billy the Kid to anyone who would listen, could this specific movie have inspired him to reach for a larger audience? Were his upcoming interviews with Morrison aimed at this particular attempt? It seems reasonable to me, but we will never know for sure.

Yes, this is speculation and not an absolute hole in Brushy's storyline and possibly mere coincidence. However, considering Brushy's relentless usage of famous names coupled with a plotline similar to the movie, I believe Lash LaRue's influence quite possible. Wouldn't you agree?

13. As discussed earlier, Brushy asserted Pat Garrett killed Billy Barlow mistaking him as Billy the Kid the night of July 14, 1881. For the sake of argument, let's indulge the pretense Pat killed someone other than Billy as true. Upon hearing gunshots, Brushy described running toward the sound, confronting Pat Garrett and deputies McKinney and Poe. Brushy maintained a gun battle ensued resulting in his receipt of three wounds. Why are there no accounts of this gun battle? Witnesses stated hearing only two gunshots that night, agreeing with the accounts of Pat Garrett and his deputies. If Brushy's allegations were true, wouldn't more than the sound of two shots have been reported by witnesses?

Let's now examine the Billy Barlow issue. Where did Brushy derive the name Billy Barlow as the person Pat Garrett allegedly killed that July night in 1881? Who was Billy Barlow? Researchers have determined the name Billy Barlow does not appear in any accounts or records during this era of Lincoln County, New Mexico history. In his interview with Morrison, Brushy provided some cover for this portion of his deception by stating the name Billy Barlow was likely an alias. By now, it should be evident Brushy favored use of names familiar to him. He often selected names of famous individuals and horses as well as versions of family names. However, Brushy's use of the name Billy Barlow has always remained a mystery.

Just what inspired Brushy to use the name of Billy Barlow? Granted, although Brushy could have just pulled a *fake* name out of thin air, I find this doubtful since Brushy consistently used names familiar to him. As a hunch, I performed an Internet search, successfully finding a character named Billy Barlow in a popular 1930s folk song. The song, "Cutty Wren," was recorded by a number of artists and groups including the Topic Singers in 1939. Most interestingly, the lyrics dealt with hunting, cutting, and the cooking of meat.

In Brushy's fable, he and Billy Barlow were hungry and a friend (Saval Gutierrez) volunteered to cook them a meal. The friend had no meat but knew of a slab of beef hanging on Pete Maxwell's porch. Brushy stated Billy Barlow departed with a butcher knife to obtain a slice of the hanging beef. According to Brushy, on this mission Billy Barlow was hunting for a cut of this meat when mistakenly killed by Pat Garrett.

I realize it is speculation Brushy borrowed the Billy Barlow name from the "Cutty Wren" recording. However, it seems plausible considering the song's main character Billy Barlow and Brushy's companion Billy Barlow were both involved with the task of hunting and cutting meat.

A portion of the lyrics of the Billy Barlow version of "Cutty Wren" follows:

"How shall we divide him?" says Risky Rob
"How shall we divide him?" says Robin to Bob
"How shall we divide him?" says Dan'l to Joe
"Hack him to pieces," says Billy Barlow
"I'll take shoulder," says Risky Rob
"I'll take side," says Robin to Bob
"I'll take back," says Dan'l to Joe
"Tail bone mine," says Billy Barlow
"How shall we cook him?" says Risky Rob

"How shall we cook him?" says Robin to Bob
"How shall we cook him?" says Dan'l to Joe
"Each as you like it," says Billy Barlow
"I'll broil shoulder" says Risky Rob
"I'll fry side," says Robin to Bob
"I'll bake back," says Dan'l to Joe
"Tail bone raw." says Billy Barlow

The timing of this popular 1939 folk recording fits well within the time frame when I believe Brushy began weaving his imaginative tale. Judge for yourself if you believe this as just another coincidence. Of course, I should again mention that at the time of the fatal shooting (Billy the Kid or someone else) in July 1881, Brushy (Oliver Pleasant Roberts) was shy of two years of age in the care of his parents in Arkansas.

14. In another Brushy confabulation pertaining to the spring of 1892 and while employed as a deputy marshal for the *U.S. Marshal Service*, Brushy asserted failing in an attempt to halt a Dalton Gang train robbery. Historical accounts indicate the Daltons heisting a total of four trains. Records do not support a Dalton Gang train robbery in the spring of 1892, but do confirm a heist later in June of the same year. Perhaps this was just a mere inaccuracy on Brushy's part, so let's assume he was referring to this June 1892 holdup. In this incident, Brushy alleged one deputy marshal (unnamed) was killed in the encounter. After researching this June heist, I found no account of a deputy killed. I suppose we are to believe the death of a U.S. marshal deputy so insignificant it went unreported. Oh wait ... I know how to reconcile this. Perhaps Brushy's details of this robbery were faulty since at that time he was 12 years old, living with his parents in Sulphur Springs, Texas.

15. Brushy stated in the Morrison interviews, "While on a cattle drive in Kansas City, I was arrested and held by the law as being Billy the Kid. The boys got me off though."

Let's think about this one. Although no specific year was given by Brushy for this event, based on the time progression of his story to Morrison, it would have occurred between 1883 and 1888. An immediate question comes to mind. What would prompt Brushy's arrest "as being Billy the Kid" when years earlier newspapers had already reported the death of the Kid from the hand of Pat Garrett? For the moment, let's take Brushy at his word. This would indicate someone recognized him as Billy the Kid. Do you really believe officials would release him without determining if they actually possessed the famous outlaw in their custody? I believe most would consider this unlikely. Of course, since Brushy (Oliver Pleasant Roberts) was born in 1879, he would have been quite safe from arrest as a young child of four to nine years of age during this time interval.

16. As previously discussed, most historically accepted research cites Catherine McCarty Antrim as the mother of Henry McCarty, aka Billy the Kid. Accommodating his genealogical confabulations, Brushy affirmed Catherine, not as his mother, but as his half aunt. Within the middle picture section of the book *Alias Billy the Kid* (Sonnichsen, Morrison, 1955), an image identified as from the Rose Collection includes the caption "Brushy Bill said this woman was Billy the Kid's aunt." From the book *The West of Billy the Kid* (Frederick Nolan, 1998), we have the following explanation regarding this image:

The original was owned by the George Griggs family, who exhibited it at their Billy the Kid Museum. It was called the Kid's mother sometime in the late 1930s, when Eugene Cunningham, author of the book Triggernometry, identified it as such to photographic collector Noah H. Rose in order to obtain from Rose another photograph. He eventually confessed that he had no idea who the woman was.

Mr. Morrison provided this same image to Brushy for his identification. Brushy obliged by identifying the lady in the photo as his half aunt, Catherine Bonney (McCarty Antrim). However, it is considered unlikely by most researchers the image was actually that of Catherine. Although incorrect identification of the image itself does not constitute an absolute hole in

Brushy's' narrative, it is clear he never met Catherine. She died in 1874, well before Brushy (Oliver Pleasant Roberts) was born in 1879.

17. During the Morrision interviews, Brushy stated:

> In the spring of 1898, Roosevelt called for volunteers for his regiment of Rough Riders. Jim and I were in Claremore about this time, so we went to Muskogee and enlisted.

In keeping with Brushy's storyline, after 1892 he reported always using one form or another of his alleged assumed identity as Oliver Roberts. Researching military service records of *Rough Rider* members, I found four volunteers with the last name of Roberts. Only one of these Roberts men enlisted in Muskogee, Indian Territory (now Oklahoma). Records indicate a 29 year old William J. Roberts enlisted in Muskogee on the 14th of May 1898.

In the spring of 1898, Brushy's actual age would have been 18. However, with his first magical age increase (birth date of December 31, 1868), Brushy's invented age would indeed calculate as 29 in the spring of 1898. As discussed earlier, I don't believe Brushy magically increased his age until 1936 for purposes of social security application. Let's overlook that for the moment and assume Brushy was using his make-believe 1868 birth year as early as 1898. Following this far-fetched theory, could William J. Roberts have been the name Brushy used supporting his claim of enlisting as a Rough Rider? This scenario would also require Brushy departing from his identity assumption of Oliver Roberts, the name (or form of name) he used on all other public records throughout his life. Could he have reverted to his invented first name of William and inserted the *J* middle initial for some unknown reason? Although Brushy had stated to Morrison he never used his birth name of William Roberts after his early teens, let's overlook this inconsistency too. Given all of these feeble assumptions, this portion of Brushy's yarn now appears at least remotely feasible.

Unfortunately, the feasibility of this scenario quickly disappears. With further research, I found military enlistment records indicating William J. Roberts was born in Georgia. His father was O. C. Roberts of Prattville,

Alabama. Additional research revealed William J. Roberts was an actual person from Alabama with a life history of his own. I believe we can now safely rule out this person as Brushy.

If Brushy's claim as a member of the Rough Riders was accurate, it would have required an alias last name. In this case, Brushy lied about using only the assumed identity of dead cousin, Ollie Roberts, after 1892. This represents a conflict in his deception either way. Of course, Brushy (Oliver Pleasant Roberts) was actually born in August 1879 and was 18 years of age during the spring of 1898, still living in his parents' home in Texas. Brushy continued to reside with his parents through the 1900 census.

18. Brushy described a horrific beating received in 1874 from his imaginary father, James Henry Roberts. Brushy reported after returning to live with his mythical father for two years, "He drew a whip from his cow horse and like to have beaten me to death. It taken me about a month to get well. My mother doctored me up." As mentioned earlier, Brushy had reported his mother dying in 1862 when he was under three years of age. In this episode it seems Brushy must have been referring to his fictional fathers' second wife, (Elizabeth Ferguson Roberts), as his mother.

Repeating from an earlier chapter, Brushy stated upon return to his imaginary father's residence he had never before met his mythical step-mother, Elizabeth Ferguson Roberts. Maybe he decided to call her mother even though he knew her only a short time. Or, could it be while telling this portion of his yarn to Morrison, he had in mind his true birth mother, Sara Elizabeth Ferguson Roberts? Brushy provided Mr. Morrison a photograph (see page 29) he identified as his mother, Mary Adeline Dunn Roberts. The picture was identified as such in the book, *Alias Billy the Kid* (Morrison, Sonnichsen, 1955). However, it is generally accepted by researchers and Roberts family members the picture actually portrays Sara Elizabeth Ferguson Roberts, Brushy's true birth mother. Again, Brushy exhibited difficulty keeping his deception consistent in the separation of his counterfeit family from his actual family.

19. According to Brushy, after healing from the terrible beating from the hands of his father, he ran away in May 1874. Brushy elaborated with details regarding his evasive escape. He asserted to have been warned by his faux father that escaping from home would be futile; the Texas Rangers would surely return him.

After re-commissioned in 1873, the Texas Rangers were a relatively small force. At this time, one could easily conclude the Texas Rangers had more important duties than locating and returning a runaway. They were incredibly busy tracking down and killing notorious criminals and desperados of the likes of bank robber Sam Bass and other outlaws. During this period of time, they were involved in the Mason County War, the Horrell-Higgins Feud, and defeating problematic stray Indian groups of Apache, Comanche, and Kiowa.

I suppose Brushy wanted us to believe his bogus father, James Henry Roberts, had considerable influence with the Texas Rangers. Of course, they would drop all other pursuits and take whatever time was necessary to find and return a 13 year old runaway. This ridiculous scenario is actually moot since Brushy (Oliver Pleasant Roberts) would not exist for another five years. Still, Brushy's elaborate escape description provided us another colorful and entertaining episode.

20. Brushy described an extraordinary experience in June 1899. Brushy recounted while he and thirty-five other cowboys were ranching in Mexico, their livestock was seized by the Mexican army. Supposedly, fifty Mexican soldiers came to round up and steal their cattle and horses. From an excerpt of this account to Morrison we have the following:

The cowboys fired into the soldiers and picked them off like blackbirds. The fourth morning when the cowboys got up, they were surrounded by almost two thousand soldiers. The cowboys agreed to fire into the soldiers' weakest spot, then make their getaway if they could. They fought for twelve days, living on wild game and trying to escape into the United States.

Brushy and thirty-five cowboys picked off fifty Mexican soldiers incurring no injuries or fatalities? While this feat was indeed impressive, the fourth morning's imagined episode was even more so. The cowboys were surrounded by two thousand Mexican soldiers. These are worse odds than at the Alamo. Thirty-six cowboys surrounded by two thousand Mexican soldiers, yet Brushy did not reveal any deaths or injuries in their successful escape. It seems rather odd for any weak spots to exist with thirty-six cowboys surrounded by two thousand Mexican soldiers, doesn't it? This must have represented an incredible escape worthy of a movie. I'll leave it to the reader to decide if this whopper can be believed. I certainly hope you laugh at this one as much as I did.

21. Another erroneous farce involves the chain of custody of the famous Billy the Kid tintype image. History records Billy as captured December 23, 1880 by Pat Garrett and his posse at Stinking Springs, New Mexico. In the Morrison interviews, Brushy related the exchange of the tintype image shortly after this capture as follows:

> The Indian was wearing a scarf that she had just made from angora goat hair. I traded her my tintype picture in my shirt pocket for this scarf.

The chain of custody of the famous tintype image has never been in question. Billy the Kid gave the tintype image to his friend, Dan Dedrick. Seven or eight years before his death in 1938, Dan gave the image to his nephew, Frank L. Upham. In 1947, Frank passed it to his sister-in-law, Elizabeth. She kept the image in a cedarwood box, later loaning it to the Lincoln County Heritage Trust in the mid-1980s. Later, the tintype image was reclaimed by the family and auctioned in 2011 for a sizable sum.

Billy the Kid.

The trade of Billy's tintype image for a scarf from an Indian lady was a touching Brushy anecdote, yet as we have learned to expect, complete fabrication. This account did, however, possess remarkable similarity to the story as related in *The Saga of Billy the Kid* published in 1925 by Walter Noble Burns. Although an untruth from Mr. Burns, it reads as follows:

> It was a cold winter's day and, as the little jail was unheated, Deluvina came home and got a heavy scarf she had knitted and took it to her hero. In return for this kindness, the Kid gave her his only photograph, which he had carried in his pocket.

Brushy's quote and Mr. Burns' fictional account are consistent. They are both, however, certainly false since the tintype actual chain of custody has been clearly established. Of note is Brushy's continued use of Mr. Burns' inaccurate accounts of events in his yarn. As previously discussed, it appears Mr. Burns influenced many Brushy confabulations of Billy the Kid history.

In reality, the historical details of this occurrence matter little regarding Brushy's touching account. In December 1880, Brushy (Oliver Pleasant Roberts) was only one year of age, cared for by his actual parents, Henry Oliver and Sara Elizabeth Ferguson Roberts.

22. After his arrest at Stinking Springs, New Mexico, Billy the Kid had no money for his court defense. All Billy owned of considerable value was his horse. In a letter to Edgar Caypless dated April 15, 1881, Billy requested his horse be sold to Scott Moore to pay Edgar Caypless' attorney fees. Unfortunately, a member of Garrett's posse, Frank Stewart, had already stolen the horse, illegally selling it to Scott Moore.

However, in the Morrison interviews, Brushy stated:

> They didn't sell my mare up at Scott Moore's in Las Vegas. He was a friend of mine, but now he said I owed him money for board.

Brushy's quote represents another departure from historically agreed accounts. The Brushy believers will likely consider this discrepancy just an insignificant error due to the foggy memory of an old man. Of course, since

Brushy (Oliver Pleasant Roberts) was just shy of three years old at the time, I conclude he must have again recalled fictive details from the wrong Billy the Kid pseudo-history source.

23. It appears Brushy believed it historically accurate Billy the Kid wore double holstered revolvers, since he avowed the same. The tintype image of Billy the Kid clearly shows only one holstered revolver. There does not appear to exist historical accounts indicating Billy ever brandished two revolvers. Brushy additionally declared fanning the hammer of his revolver during gunfights. I would consider this unlikely due to the obvious loss in accuracy. Still, movie westerns of Brushy's day often showed gunslingers wearing two revolvers or fanning the hammer of one. After all, Roy Rogers, in his movies, often wore a double holstered set (including in a movie where he portrayed Billy the Kid). A number of Billy the Kid movies have shown double holstered revolvers or fanning the hammer in shootouts. I suspect western movies contributed to Brushy's inspiration to weave these colorful anecdotes within his fantasy.

24. Brushy's failed attempt in November 1950 to obtain a pardon from Governor Mabry (promised Billy by Governor Wallace in 1880) was by all accounts a ridiculous media event. Brushy, without the benefit of his composition notebooks, could not satisfy even the simplest of questions asked. In the prologue of *Alias Billy the Kid* (Sonnichsen, Morrison, 1955), Mr. Sonnichesen stated:

> Roberts made a poor showing. He couldn't remember Pat Garrett's name. He couldn't remember the places they asked him about. When Will Robinson asked him if he killed Bell and Olinger when he escaped from the Lincoln jail, he said he didn't do any shooting - just got on his horse and rode off.

I believe you can see a couple of difficulties from the above excerpt. Failing to remember Pat Garrett's name is a bit surprising, isn't it? How about the part where Brushy proclaimed not killing Deputies Bell and Olinger, while all historical accounts clearly affirm Billy the Kid killed both in his escape? Well, actually Brushy was telling the truth about not killing Deputies

Bell and Olinger. At that time in 1881, Brushy (Oliver Pleasant Roberts) was a sixteen month old infant living at home in Arkansas with his parents, Henry Oliver and Sara Elizabeth Ferguson Roberts.

Brushy while awaiting a meeting with New Mexico Governor Mabry in November, 1950. Pencil sketch by Linda Weatherman.

Affidavits Obtained by Morrison and Brushy

William V. Morrison expended considerable effort contacting individuals who alleged personal knowledge regarding Brushy or Billy the Kid. These endeavors focused on obtaining affidavits Morrison believed to support Brushy's claim as Billy the Kid.

1. Morrison and Brushy arrived in Carlsbad, New Mexico, meeting brothers Sam and William Jones. Sam and William were brothers of John and Jim Jones, who both worked with Billy the Kid at the Chisum Ranch and fought in the Lincoln County War. After a long talk with Sam and William, Morrison's request for signed affidavits was denied with Sam stating Brushy gave no conclusive proof of his claim. Morrison and Brushy failed in their attempt to obtain affidavits from the two brothers. Even if they had been successful, I can see little value in confirmations from individuals who had never met Billy. It appears to me this attempt by Morrison and Brushy was a worthless endeavor, unworthy of inclusion in the pro-Brushy book *Alias Billy the Kid* (Sonnichsen, Morrison, 1955).

2. Morrison and Brushy achieved more success with Mr. DeWitt Travis, a Longview, Texas oil man. Mr. Travis contended knowing Brushy from boyhood and had always been certain Brushy was Billy the Kid. He signed an affidavit to that effect. From *Alias Billy the Kid*, Mr. DeWitt Travis stated:

> My father Elbert Travis and Brushy Bill's father served together under Quantrill during the Civil War. My mother Martha Ann Patterson and Brushy Bill's mother were girlhood friends—in fact, friends throughout life. With this background, I have known Brushy Bill intimately all my life.

Considerable difficulty exists with Mr. Travis' statement concluding Brushy was Billy the Kid. To begin with, Brushy's alleged father, James Henry

Roberts, did not exist. Perhaps Mr. Travis was referring to Brushy's actual father, Henry Oliver Roberts. However, that can't be since Brushy's father, Henry Oliver Roberts, was born in 1852. He would have been too young to have served in the Civil War and certainly was not a member of Quantrill's Raiders.

After modest research, I discovered Dewitt Travis' father, Elbert Travis, served in the Confederate Calvary during the Civil War. He enlisted August 14, 1864 in Mississippi serving with the 3rd Battalion of the Mississippi Calvary. He was taken prisoner and paroled May 16, 1865 at Columbus, Mississippi. It does not appear DeWitt Travis' father served within proximity to the William Quantrill command at any time during the Civil War. This portion of Mr. Travis' quote was inaccurate as was his statement Brushy's imaginary or actual father served with his father, Elbert Travis.

I have no reason to doubt Mr. Travis's mother, Martha Ann Patterson Travis, was a girlhood friend to Brushy's (Oliver Pleasant Roberts') mother. After all, Brushy's mother was Sara Elizabeth Ferguson Roberts, wife of Henry Oliver Roberts. Sara would have been within two years of Martha's age. The Henry Oliver Roberts family resided in Van Zandt County, Texas at the same time as the Elbert Travis family. Per Brushy's story, however, his fairy tale mother, Mary Adeline Dunn Roberts, died when Brushy was under three years of age in Buffalo Gap, Texas. It is clear that Martha Ann Patterson Travis did not know Brushy's alleged mother since she never existed. By Mr. Travis' own admission, his mother knew Brushy's mother throughout life. For this to have been true, logic dictates Mr. Travis was referring to Brushy's actual mother, Sara Elizabeth Ferguson Roberts. This would, in effect, further support Brushy's true identity as Oliver Pleasant Roberts.

I have another difficulty with Mr. Travis' statements. After already stating his mother knew Brushy's mother throughout life, I see a bit of a generational problem. At the time of Brushy's death, he purported an age of 90, while at this time, Mr. Travis would have been less than 60; yet, their respective mothers were supposedly girlhood friends. Of course, since Brushy was actually only 71 at the time of his death in 1950, this would certainly be more believable. The conclusion drawn from this would certainly indicate

Mr. Travis was again referring to Sara Elizabeth Ferguson Roberts, the actual mother of Brushy (Oliver Pleasant Roberts).

Mr. Travis quoted to Morrison in 1951, "Ollie's mother and father died thinking Brushy was their son ... but he was not." This statement appears to be additional icing on the cake. First, Mr. Travis contradicts the father-mother-son relationship he previously established. Secondly, it conflicts with the earlier statement of Mr. Travis claiming his mother knew Brushy's mother throughout life. Mr. Travis' credibility is erased due to his own contradictions. I suppose true Brushy believers will continue to attempt to explain such difficulties. One must always be aware of Brushy believer creativity.

How could Mr. Travis think Brushy was Billy the Kid? Could it be Brushy told him so and that was good enough? Keep in mind, Brushy told Morrison he never told anyone he was Billy the Kid (including his wives) until the time of his first interview in 1949 (not true, of course). I am only surprised Mr. Morrison chose to include this worthless affidavit as positive supporting evidence for Brushy's claim.

3. Morrison and Brushy visited old-timers, Luis Martinez and Hernando Chavez, in El Paso, Texas. These individuals stated that to the best of their knowledge Billy the Kid lived in Mexico after his supposed death in 1881. Chavez also claimed he was told by some unidentified person that Billy the Kid fought with Carranza and Pancho Villa during the Mexican Revolution.

So, just what do we have with this account? We have a couple of old-timers believing Billy the Kid was not killed by Pat Garrett in 1881. Although many have this belief, what exactly does this have to do with proving Brushy was Billy the Kid? As stated earlier, I am not examining whether or not Billy the Kid was killed by Pat Garrett in 1881, only Brushy's claim of being Billy the Kid. I noticed there was nothing mentioned in these two old-timers' accounts confirming they believed Brushy was the historical outlaw. I wonder why they would not agree to sign an affidavit to that effect. Could it be they had never even met Billy the Kid? What a wasted effort this interview was.

4. Morrison and Brushy visited Severo Gallegos of Ruidoso, New Mexico. Supposedly, Severo was a child playing marbles under a tree in Lincoln during the time Billy the Kid killed deputies Olinger and Bell. In this case, they were

visiting with someone who, as a child, might actually have met Billy the Kid some 70 years earlier.

Initially, Severo simply stated Brushy was not old enough to be Billy the Kid. This seems to have been an obvious observation since Severo would have been older than Oliver Pleasant Roberts, Brushy's true identity. After some convincing by Morrison, Severo decided to examine Brushy's eyes for specks. After a careful viewing, Severo changed his mind stating, "Only Billy had eyes like that." He was now ready to sign an affidavit confirming Brushy was the true Billy the Kid. He based his certainty simply due to some specks in Brushy's eyes. Morrison mentioned he had not noticed the spots in Brushy's eyes or knew of any significance of any such spots. This identity confirmation appears all too unconvincing. I believe the most important statement made by Servero was his initial impression of Brushy as too young to have been Billy. What do you think?

Brushy and Billy Facial Comparisons

Brushy believers insist facial comparisons to the famous tintype image of Billy the Kid are significant proof of Brushy's claim. Although I know with certainty Brushy was not Billy the Kid, some authors and amateur researchers have considered results of facial comparison studies definitive. I've summarized the results from the two major studies as follows:

A 1987 study sponsored by The Lincoln County Heritage Trust was performed by physicist Dr. Thomas G. Kyle with the Los Alamos National Laboratory in New Mexico. After considerable computer image facial feature analysis, Dr. Kyle concluded Brushy's facial features were not a match to the tintype image of Billy the Kid. One major factor in arriving at this conclusion was a vast difference in chin structure. Brushy's chin was flat while the chin of Billy the Kid was pointed. Even to the untrained eye, the chins show little similarity. The study by Dr. Kyle also indicated significant differences based on eye position, nose, and ears. Dr. Kyle's overall conclusion was Brushy was not the same person as shown in the tintype image of Billy the Kid.

Brushy believers point to issues they believe problematic with this study. The first issue cited was lack of sophistication of the computer analysis. They consider the analysis deficient, believing the study was filled with errors and misinterpretation. The second issue noted pertains to a conflict of interest, contending The Lincoln County Heritage Trust desired a negative comparison outcome. Brushy believers have accused this organization of influencing the results as an attempt to retain the status quo legend of Billy the Kid in favor of New Mexico tourism interests.

A later 1990 study was performed by Scott T. Acton at the Laboratory for Vision Systems and Advanced Graphics, University of Texas at Austin. This statistical Acton Study did not conclude Brushy and Billy the Kid were the same man, but indicated some similarity. Statistical analysis showed a lower mean squared error (MSE) of 17.7. An exact match would yield a MSE error of 0.0. Brushy believers have explained the MSE error rate by proclaiming one would not expect an exact facial image match of an alleged 89 year old Brushy (actually only 69 years of age) with the tintype image of Billy the Kid at about twenty years of age. The overall results from this study were summarized as inconclusive.

In regard to Brushy vs Billy teeth structure, Billy the Kid was known by witnesses as having protruding front teeth, a characteristic apparent in the tintype image. At the time of the Morrison interviews, Brushy was toothless with all teeth having been removed in the 1930s by a dentist in Gladewater, Texas. However, Brushy presented Morrison a number of photos of himself at a younger age brandishing teeth. None of the aforementioned images exhibited any sign of protruding front teeth. Why is that? I patiently await a Brushy believer explanation for this incongruency.

Brushy believer authors have published significant details regarding facial comparisons. Having only lightly summarized results, I personally consider this topic of little importance. Believing I have already provided overwhelming evidence Brushy was not the legendary Billy the Kid, I consider the senseless discussion of facial features as moot and unimportant. However, for those desiring the entertainment of more detail, I would recommend *The Return of the Outlaw Billy the Kid* (1998) by Brushy believer author W. C. Jameson. In his book, Mr. Jameson included an entire chapter detailing so-called similarities in facial features between two very different individuals. Such creativity could likely result in the conclusion Marilyn Monroe and Mona Lisa were the same person.

Brushy and Billy Handwriting Comparisons

Morrison indicated Brushy as semi-literate, with writings in his notebooks resembling hen scratch. While examining Billy's writings, however, one sees relatively neat flowing cursive handwriting complete with well-constructed sentences.

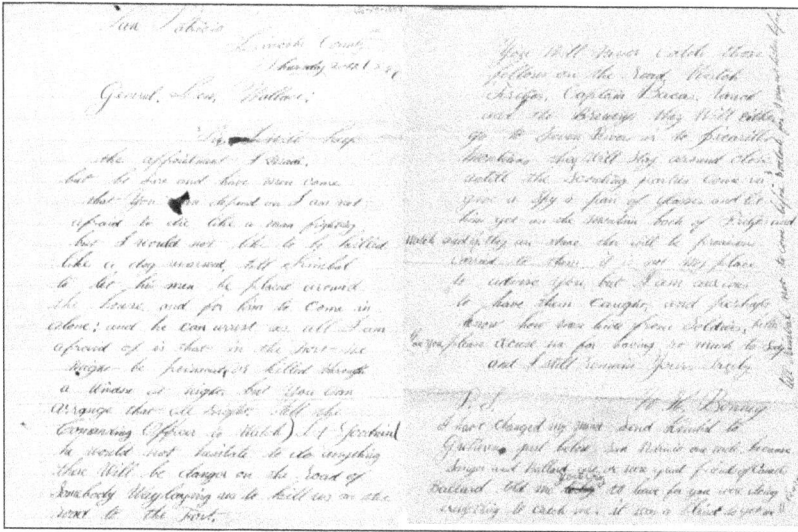

The two-page letter Billy wrote to Governor Wallace illustrating excellent penmanship. Image courtesy of the Fray Angélico Chávez History Library, New Mexico History Museum.

If interested in viewing Brushy's handwriting, a sample may be found with an internet search (websites have lesser copyright usage standards than print publications). An example of Brushy's handwriting from a letter he penned to Mrs. Ola Everhard may be viewed on the Brushy Bill/Billy the Kid Message Board website under "Brushy's Handwriting," (Land).

Brushy believers will excuse the vast difference in handwriting quality due to Brushy's advanced age of 90 (while in fact, Oliver Pleasant Roberts was only 71 at the time of his letter to Mrs. Ola Everhard). Yes, penmanship can certainly diminish with age, but the discrepancy appears extreme. Additionally, Brushy believers will claim Billy's letters to Governor Wallace were not penned by Billy or insist the Brushy letter to Mrs. Everhard was written by his wife.

By Brushy's own admission, much of his correspondence and signatures on legal documents were performed by his wives. Brushy's signatures certainly appear different on various recorded documents. Researchers have performed extensive signature studies attempting to determine which were actually those of Brushy. It appears only educated guesses rather than definitive conclusions exist.

Further complicating the issue of Brushy's handwriting is the statement by an unidentified second cousin of Brushy. In a letter to Mr. Tunstill appearing on page 35 of his book, *Billy the Kid and Me Were the Same*, this cousin stated Brushy could not read or write, often signing papers with an X. Other details in the letter appear to be accurate and it is clear this unidentified cousin was referring to Brushy as Oliver Pleasant Roberts. While I do believe Brushy could read and write, it is quite plausible some of his signed documents did not bear his signature and were signed with an X or by a wife.

Arguments regarding Brushy and Billy handwriting comparisons will likely continue for many years into the future. Experts have found negligible similarities between Brushy's handwriting and Billy the Kid's. I believe the significance of this topic unimportant as I have already provided the reader overwhelming disproof of Brushy's Billy the Kid claim without need of the unrewarding effort of further handwriting analysis.

Brushy's vs Billy's Wounds and Scars

Much has been discussed in regard to alleged scars exhibited by Brushy. When first meeting with Brushy, Morrison desired proof of scarring from Billy the Kid's past wounds. Brushy was more than happy to accommodate, with Mr. Morrison counting twenty-six scars from alleged bullet and knife wounds.

Other than the shot from Pat Garrett supposedly killing Billy in 1881, historical accounts reflect Billy the Kid was grazed by bullets no more than three times with no reported knife wounds. On the day of the ambush of Sheriff William Brady, Billy was grazed by a bullet resulting in a hip flesh wound. The second reported incident was at Blazer's Mill. Billy received an arm flesh wound from a shot fired by Buckshot Roberts. A third incident which might have possibly resulted in a wounding of Billy was during his escape from the burning McSween house at the end of the five-day Battle of Lincoln. Although historical accounts indicate no other times Billy was wounded, there could have been others.

Of the occurrences listed above, Brushy did not mention the Blazer's Mill episode. He only attributed scars to wounds allegedly received during the ambush of Brady, during his escape from the burning McSween house, and his imaginary gunfight with Pat Garrett and deputies at Fort Sumner. Surely, Brushy could have accredited more of his many asserted gunshot and knife wounds. Could it be incidents of additional Billy the Kid wounds were just not reported in the books Brushy read?

I do not doubt the quantity of Brushy's scars Mr. Morrison tabulated. Since other evidence I have already provided substantiates Brushy was not Billy the Kid, the logical conclusion is he obtained these scars by happenstance during 70 years of lifetime experiences. According to census records, Oliver Roberts listed his occupation as farmer. Although not for certain, it is quite possible Brushy participated in rodeo events during his lifetime. Farming and rodeo activities often result in frequent injuries. It would not be uncommon for one to have a number of cuts and marks from such a life. I believe many of us can count ten or more scars from accidents and medical procedures during our lives. I know I can.

The ruins at Blazer's Mill, New Mexico. Photograph from 1893 at the location of a bloody gunfight on April 1, 1878.

Brushy and J. Frank Dalton. Fraud by Association?

In the latter years of his life, a man identified as J. Frank Dalton proclaimed himself as Jesse James. Mr. Dalton died August 15, 1951, less than a year after Brushy's death. Brushy reported knowing Jessie James for 78 years and declared the individual identified as J. Frank Dalton was actually the legendary Jesse James. Mr. Dalton kindly returned the favor exclaiming Brushy as Billy the Kid. A photo shoot arranged by Morrison of Brushy with Mr. Dalton occurred September 6, 1949. The images and imaginative claims reported made interesting newspaper press, capturing the imagination of many.

The validity of J. Frank Dalton's claim has been debated over the years, similar to that of Brushy. Mr. Dalton alleged the man killed and buried as Jesse James was actually a man named Charlie Bigelow. Brushy attempted enhancing Dalton's account by avouching his imaginary father, Wild Henry (James Henry) Roberts, helped Jesse by intentionally misidentifying Bigelow's body as Jesse James. A fabricated person killed in Jesse James' place appears amazingly similar to Brushy's concocted story of fictive Billy Barlow killed in lieu of Billy the Kid. Could it be since Brushy and J. Frank Dalton were mutually professed long-time friends, they compared notes while constructing their fantasies?

I will not delve into detail regarding the J. Frank Dalton debate as it is not the subject of my book. If interested, however, a number of books and articles have been written on this topic. Suffice it to say, J. Frank's declaration of himself as Jesse James did not hold up under questioning from Jesse James' surviving relatives. An exhumation of remains marked as J. Frank Dalton was performed May 30, 2000 for purposes of a DNA comparison. The results were negative, yet sparked another debate whether the correct remains were tested. It is generally accepted by most researchers and historians J. Frank Dalton was not Jesse James.

J. Frank Dalton (left) with Brushy. Pencil sketch by Linda Weatherman.

How do we evaluate the mutual acknowledgments of Brushy and J. Frank Dalton as famous outlaws? I have found no historical accounts where Billy the Kid ever met Jesse James. It does not appear the two individuals were ever in the same location at the same time. The only accounts of Jesse and Billy meeting are from Brushy's own fable. It would also be difficult for Brushy to have known J. Frank Dalton for seventy-eight years since, at the time of his statement, Brushy was only seventy years of age. I would consider his confirmation J. Frank Dalton as Jesse James a bit suspect, wouldn't you?

If Brushy or J. Frank Dalton was a real deal famous outlaw, do you think either would acknowledge a pretender? Researchers have already deemed J. Frank Dalton a fake and I have already provided overwhelming evidence proving Brushy a fake to any logical person's satisfaction. Doesn't it make more sense to believe that both were imposters? If still not convinced of the invalidity of Brushy's Billy the Kid claim, maybe my upcoming chapters will convince you. If not, you are certainly one of the true believers and there is little hope you will change your mind regardless of evidence and logic to the contrary.

Uncle Kit Carson. Role model for Brushy?

While researching, I discovered an item of interest regarding Brushy's close relationship with a recognized storyteller. The book, *Legendary Locals of Roswell* (John Lemay, Roger K. Burnett, 2012), contains a chapter titled "Uncle Kit Carson, Father of Billy the Kid." Within this chapter, photos illustrate an interesting individual decked out in an *Old West* style buckskin outfit, known as Uncle Kit Carson. His true name was Oran Ardious Woodman, born December 30, 1870, in Zanesville, Illinois. It appears Orin performed as Uncle Kit Carson, as well as Kit Carson in Buffalo Bill's Wild West Show during the 1900-1906 era.

Subsequent to Uncle Kit's death in 1957, a letter was found in his belongings dated April 1, 1949, signed by O. L. Roberts (Brushy used the O. L. derivation of his name in the latter years of his life). Brushy addressed Uncle Kit as dad, implying a close relationship, although certainly not genetic. I have not obtained an actual copy of this particular letter, but located a transcription of the text provided by William A. Tunstill within his correspondence with my mother, Eulaine Haws. At the time Brushy penned this letter, he was visiting friends in Dora, New Mexico; it was two months before has first interview with Morrison. The content of Tunstill's transcription of the letter is as follows:

> Dear Uncle Kit Carson,
>
> We got here O.K. We are doing fine. Hope this finds you the same. The wind blows every day and it is cold - Wheat looks good, good season in the ground. Cattle they are fat, they sure look good. Lots of cattle here. We heard from the boys over sea. (Note: This is believed to be a reference to nephews in the Army.) They are moving four hundred miles farther north from where they are.

We heard from Billie the Kid. He is doing fine and we are looking for him to come visit us in Hico, Texas. He will stay with us two weeks, then he will go and stay for three years, Dad. I will do my best to get Billie the Kid to come by and see you. We sure are lonesome and sure are blue about our boys. Sure wish they was at home.

Well Dad, here is hoping you the very best of luck and I will be over that way when the fruit gets ripe. Here is hoping we live in peace a long time. May God bless you in your old days.

Love and best wishes to you from your son,

O. L. Roberts

April 1, 1949

As previously stated, Brushy's letter to Uncle Kit Carson was just a couple of months before his first interview with Morrison in June 1949. I note two observations from Brushy's letter. First, I find it incredibly interesting Brushy mentioned Billy the Kid was coming to visit him for two weeks. How could this be with Brushy claiming he was Billy the Kid? Secondly, it is obvious from the affectionate terms *dad* and *from your son*, a close relationship existed between Brushy and Uncle Kit. Of course, Mr. Tunstill had an explanation by speculating Brushy was talking in code to Uncle Kit. Tunstill even penned the words "cover-up" on the transcription he provided my mother. I consider it more likely, however, Brushy was arranging an upcoming visit with Uncle Kit to help with final touches to his fable.

I now feel it pertinent to include a few details regarding the possible influence of this colorful individual known as Uncle Kit Carson. Let's begin with an article earlier referenced from *Legendary Locals of Roswell* that stated, "Uncle Kit was neither the father of O. L. Roberts nor the relative of Kit Carson, just an eccentric circus performer who loved to tell stories."

At the time of this writing, a summary of Uncle Kit's life (author unknown) appeared on the website for Heritage Auctions. This summary includes the quote:

Whichever identity captures your fancy, several facts remain. Uncle Kit was definitely knowledgeable and experienced with Indians, frontier life, and was a regular performer in various Wild West shows, circuses, and rodeos, including Buffalo Bill's Wild West. The ultimate performer, he actually became the character he was playing at the time and was able to fool a lot of people, even after his death.

Heritage Auctions also included a post pertaining to the auction sale of Uncle Kit Carson's belongings. This same post included an interesting excerpt (author unknown) pertaining to details of Uncle Kit Carson's life:

This older gentleman told amazing stories about his birth in New Mexico in 1858 to Kit Carson's half brother William and his wife Maria, about being an Army scout, a cattle drover for John Chisum, a personal friend of Billy the Kid, a participant with Teddy Roosevelt in the Spanish American War, appearing with Buffalo Bill and Pawnee Bill Wild West shows, and the list goes on … It was not until sometime after his death that the known story of Uncle Kit's life started unraveling.

From the book titled *Treasures of History IV - Historical Events of Chaves County, NM* (Fleming, 2003) we have the following quote from Mabel Pittman Hickerson, a relative of Uncle Kit (Oran Woodman), who knew him during his life:

He had traveled with the Wild West shows and I being a kid, that fascinated me. And he told us stories. For years he claimed he was the real Kit Carson. This suggests he started calling himself Kit Carson soon after his wife left him, probably between 1911 and 1920. None of that stuff about living with the Indians and being a guide was true.

"Uncle Kit" Carson. Pencil sketch by Linda Weatherman.

It appears Brushy and Uncle Kit had much in common. I will list some of the amazing similarities in their respective claimed life experiences:

1. Brushy and Uncle Kit knew each other as evidenced by the letter from Brushy found in Uncle Kit's possessions.

2. Uncle Kit claimed to be the real Kit Carson at times, while other times the nephew of Kit Carson. Uncle Kit claimed to be a personal friend of Billy the Kid. Brushy, however, claimed to be Billy the Kid and that his fictional father, James Henry Roberts, was a friend and associate of the historical Kit Carson.

3. They both changed their year of birth (Brushy from 1879 to 1859 and Uncle Kit from 1870 to 1858) to appropriately belong to the era fitting their respective fables.

4. They both claimed past employment at the Chisum Ranch.

5. They both claimed participation as a Rough Rider in the Spanish American War.

6. They both claimed past employment as a scout (Uncle Kit for the U.S. Calvary and Brushy for a stagecoach line).

7. They both claimed past employment with Buffalo Bill's Wild West Show.

8. They both claimed past employment with the Pawnee Bill Wild West Show.

9. They both claimed past employment as a deputy marshal in the Oklahoma Territory.

10. They both were known by family and others as storytellers.

The similarities between Brushy and Uncle Kit abound. Although not definitive, could Brushy's affectionate association with the circus performer and storyteller, Uncle Kit, have aided him in weaving portions of his fanciful fable? I consider it quite feasible, yet will leave judgment to the reader. If nothing else, I find Brushy's association with this colorful character interesting, especially considering Brushy's false tale in an earlier chapter involving his fictional father with Kit Carson and Custer.

Christopher "Kit" Houston Carson, 1809–1868.

Governor Wallace's Promised Pardon

Although it was not my intent to delve substantially into Governor Lew Wallace's promised pardon and subsequent trial of Billy the Kid in 1879, I believe it appropriate to point out a few of Brushy's historically inaccurate statements.

1. Regarding the pardon promised Billy by Governor Lew Wallace, Brushy stated in the Morrison interviews, "He promised to pardon me if I would stand trial on my indictments in the district court in Lincoln, testify before the grand jury in the Chapman case, and testify against Dudley."

Governor Lew Wallace. Illustration from *Harper's Weekly,* March 6, 1886.

This was not the deal promised Billy by Governor Lew Wallace. The arrangement between Governor Wallace and Billy was quite different. In exchange for Billy allowing his arrest and providing testimony pertaining to the Huston Chapman murder, he would subsequently be relieved from standing trial for the Sheriff Brady murder. After Billy's testimony, per the arrangement, charges were not dropped as promised by Governor Wallace. Some accounts reflect the district attorney, William L. Rynerson, simply disregarded the Governor's orders to set Billy free. Whether it was Governor Wallace breaking his word or the district attorney disregarding orders, Billy went on trial for the murder of Sheriff Brady. This resulted in the kangaroo court outcome controlled by the Santa Fe Ring. Billy was found guilty and sentenced to hang by the neck until dead.

Considering the importance of the pardon agreement, it would seem peculiar Brushy would not remember the details of this notorious arrangement. Naturally, since Brushy was not Billy the Kid and only read inaccurate details published by pseudo-history authors, it really isn't surprising. After all, many writings falsely indicated Billy had agreed to stand trial for the murder of Sheriff Brady.

2. Although in conflict with an earlier statement during the Morrison interviews, Brushy stated: "I heard that Governor Wallace had offered a thousand dollars for me if I would come in and testify. I wrote and told him that I would come in if he would annul those indictments against me." Actually this is closer to the real agreement Billy made with Governor Wallace. However, the thousand dollars was an amount Billy mentioned in the letter he wrote to Governor Wallace as the price on his head offered for his capture, not an amount to be paid Billy for testifying. It is amazing how Brushy misrepresented coming in vs capture and confusing who actually would be rewarded with a prize of a thousand dollars.

3. In regard to the trial of Billy the Kid for the killing of Sheriff Brady, Brushy, in his interview with Morrison, stated, "Old Dad" Peppin (George W. Peppin) testified at my trial in Mesilla that I killed Brady." In actuality, however, only circumstantial evidence was introduced during the trial. No witness testified Billy the Kid had killed Brady. This was just one more inaccurate statement provided by Brushy.

Brushy believers will write off his inaccuracies as minor fuzzy lapses in an old man's recollection of events or even more likely never compared his confabulations with accepted historical accounts. Of course, the real reason

Brushy didn't have accurate details was because he wasn't involved. At the time of Billy's trial in 1881, Brushy (Oliver Pleasant Roberts) was an infant under two years of age in the care of his parents in Arkansas.

MORE FALSE DOCUMENTATION FROM MR. TUNSTILL

Early during the Morrison interviews, Brushy stated his grandfather was Ben Roberts. He further reported Ben settling in Nacogdoches, Texas in 1835 and assisting Sam Houston in liberating Texas from Mexico during the Texas Revolution.

In an earlier chapter, I documented Brushy's grandfather as Joseph Roberts (page 28), thus disproving Brushy's claim his grandfather was Ben or Benjamin Roberts. I broach this topic again in response to a misleading document provided by Mr. Tunstill in his book *Billy the Kid and Me Were the Same*. On page 99, Mr. Tunstill provided a land grant document dated April 18, 1850, issued by the State of Texas to Benjamin Roberts, for 640 acres of land in Navarro County, Texas.

At the bottom of the page, Mr. Tunstill included the following statement:

> Note: Benjamin Roberts, grandfather of Ollie Brushy Bill Roberts, received 640 acres of land for his services in the army for active duty in the Texas Revolution in 1835-1836. No money was available; therefore, the land certificates were issued by the Texas Republic.

First, I would like to address the obvious. Mr. Tunstill's statement the land certificate was "issued by the Texas Republic" is in error. As illustrated below, the land grant was issued from the State of Texas, not the Republic of Texas. The land grant was issued April 18, 1850, well after Texas gained statehood in 1845.

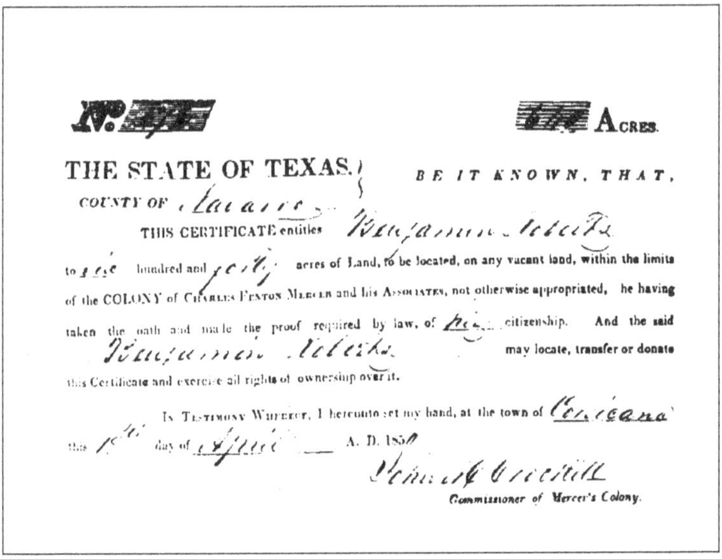

No. [redacted] [redacted] Acres.

THE STATE OF TEXAS, } COUNTY OF Navarro } BE IT KNOWN, THAT, THIS CERTIFICATE entitles Benjamin Roberts to six hundred and forty acres of Land, to be located, on any vacant land, within the limits of the COLONY of CHARLES FENTON MERCER and his ASSOCIATES, not otherwise appropriated, he having taken the oath and made the proof required by law, of his citizenship. And the said Benjamin Roberts may locate, transfer or donate this Certificate and exercise all rights of ownership over it.

IN TESTIMONY WHEREOF, I hereunto set my hand, at the town of Corsicana this 18th day of April A. D. 1850

John Crockett
Commissioner of Mercer's Colony.

I found records of a Benjamin Roberts I believe to be the person referenced in the land grant document. This Benjamin Roberts was born in Illinois in 1818 and died September 1870. His tombstone lies in the Ward Cemetery, Corsicana, Navarro County, Texas, the same county referenced in the 640 acre land grant certificate. Thinking this could have been just a coincidence since Roberts is a common name, I obtained further research results for this Benjamin Roberts from the Daughters of the Republic of Texas on Ancestry.com. As of October 20, 2014, a posting involving this Roberts family was found at the following web address: www.rootsweb.ancestry.com/~txccmdrt/roberts_benjamin.htm

The posting reads as follows:

> Benjamin came to the Republic of Texas in 1841. He was issued an unconditional certificate #380 for 320 acres by the Board of Land Commissioners in Washington County, Texas on 29 June 1846. He applied for and received land in Hill, McLennan, or Navarro County. He chose land in Navarro County. He received 640 acres on 18 April 1850 certificate #176, which is signed by John Crockett, Commissioner for the Mercer Colony. The rest of

the Roberts clan, two brothers, wives and children came to Texas with his wife Anna Lemley Roberts in 1846.

The certificate date and number illustrated on the previous page, as well as provided in Mr. Tunstill's book, agrees precisely with the Roberts family posting. It's safe to conclude we have the correct Benjamin Roberts. This Benjamin Roberts, however, has nothing more than the same name in common with Brushy's fictional grandfather, Ben. I suppose Mr. Tunstill thought if he found anyone with the same name in historical records, it would aid in supporting the genealogical portion of Brushy's unbelievable yarn. Then again, this sort of substantiating proof by Mr. Tunstill has ceased to surprise me. I'll discuss this further for those that believe this Benjamin Roberts could be the individual of Brushy's imaginary ancestry.

Contrary to Mr. Tunstill's claim the land allowance was due to service in the Texas War of Independence, this land grant was simply awarded for settling in the Republic of Texas. I researched the conditions required for land awards during this time. An allowance of 640 acres per family head was granted to residents who immigrated to Texas between January 1, 1840 and January 2, 1842. The Benjamin Roberts of this discussion settled in Texas in 1841, thus qualifying for this acreage. The land award to this Benjamin Roberts had nothing to do with "his services in the army for active duty in the Texas Revolution in 1835-1836," as Mr. Tunstill stated.

Now, for the benefit of any remaining Brushy believers, I went ahead and researched the descendants of this Benjamin Roberts. His three sons were Evan (b.1839), Jacob R. (b. 1845), and J. M. (b.1853). Brushy stated his father was James Henry Roberts, born in 1832. This adequately proves the Benjamin Roberts referenced in this chapter was not the grandfather Brushy claimed.

One more detail from my research is perhaps worth mentioning. Although a number of Roberts names appear as serving in the Texas Revolution, I did not locate a Ben or Benjamin Roberts. The only record I found with any mention of a Benjamin Roberts during this time period was from a document dated October 18, 1844. The content of this document involves the sale of 794 pounds of beef and includes the names of Sam Houston and Benjamin

Roberts. This quite possibly could be the aforementioned Benjamin Roberts settling in the Republic of Texas in 1841 (before Texas statehood in 1845); but I don't know for sure. By this point, it really doesn't matter as this entire discussion quickly becomes moot. There does not exist a Benjamin Roberts accommodating Brushy's fable as his grandfather. In an earlier chapter, I have already provided proof the grandfather of Brushy (Oliver Pleasant Roberts) was Joseph Roberts.

I included this chapter to further illustrate an additional ridiculous attempt by Mr. Tunstill to accommodate portions of Brushy's fable. I hope you too have discovered the pattern by now. Brushy created imaginative fiction. Mr. Tunstill attempted to prove the fiction as factual with any straw of unconnected documentation, no matter how unrelated or false. Compounding the falsehoods, additional authors and researchers arrived on the scene after publication of Mr. Tunstill's book in 1988. They assumed his false claims as fact, and continued, through their own works, to mislead the general public into believing Brushy was Billy the Kid. It's really sad, don't you think? As many have said, fiction outsells non-fiction. Fictional books are entertaining, yet it is quite unfortunate when fiction writers choose to market their works as non-fiction.

More So-Called Brushy Believer Proof

Brushy believers have continued using a specific published witness claim as proof Brushy was Billy the Kid. While traveling with his imaginary friend, Mountain Bill, Brushy described working a few months at the Gila Ranch in Arizona beginning early April 1877. Years later, after Billy's supposed death on July 14, 1881 at the hands of Pat Garrett, Brushy asserted participating in Buffalo Bill's Wild West Show.

In August 1929, an article was published in a short-lived publication titled Texas Monthly (not to be confused with the current magazine of that name). Within the article, Cyclone Denton was interviewed by Ramon Adams. Mr. Denton professed working with Billy the Kid at the Gila Ranch and later (after Billy's supposed death in 1881) riding for Buffalo Bill with Billy.

The believers jumped on this statement by Cyclone Denton as further proof Brushy was indeed Billy the Kid. Brushy claimed working at the Gila Ranch and Buffalo Bill's Wild West Show, consistent with Mr. Denton's account of his experience with Billy. There are a couple of problems with this so-called proof, however. First, let's assume for the moment Pat Garrett did not kill Billy the Kid and what Mr. Denton said in his interview was true. Does this mean Brushy was Billy the Kid? Of course it doesn't. Even if Mr. Denton's statements were true, it would only indicate Billy the Kid did not meet his demise July 14, 1881. This certainly would not in any way prove Brushy was Billy. Secondly, how do we know Mr. Denton wasn't mistaken or perhaps not telling the truth? We don't. As we all know, it is not uncommon for folks to falsely tell others they knew or were in the presence of famous individuals during their lifetime.

So how did Brushy know of an alleged employment of Billy at the Arizona Gila Ranch? The *Texas Monthly* article referenced was published August 1929, just a relatively short while before I believe Brushy began his elaborate myth construction. Wherever Brushy obtained this information is actually moot. In April 1877, when Cyclone Denton claimed working with Billy the Kid on the Gila Ranch, more than two years remained before Brushy's birth as Oliver Pleasant Roberts in August 1879.

THE THEORY OF TWO OLIVERS

The theory of two Olivers is an extremely convoluted proposal by a specific Brushy believer, concocted in an attempt to validate portions of Brushy's hoax. This is one of the more complicated suppositions and if already convinced of the invalidity of Brushy's claims (as you should be), you may certainly skip to my In Conclusion chapter. However, if you are open to additional entertainment you might enjoy this rather complicated and irrational speculation.

A familiar practice among Brushy believers is to continually relate improbable explanations for Brushy's falsehoods. Initial difficulties to overcome by the believers are his age claim, identity assumption of cousin Ollie, and lifetime derivative use of the name Oliver Pleasant Roberts. Even after attempting to overcome these difficulties, believers should have found themselves confronted with entwined contradictions.

As promised in an earlier chapter, I will discuss one of the more far out theories speculating Brushy's claimed identity assumption of cousin Ollie was of an Oliver L. Roberts rather than Oliver Pleasant Roberts. This theory was proposed by Mr. Wayne Land. Mr. Land administers the Brushy Bill/Billy the Kid Message Board on the web. One of his scenarios portrays two men named Oliver, both sons of Henry Oliver Roberts and Sara Elizabeth Ferguson Roberts. Mr. Land contends there might have existed an elder son named Oliver L., born out of wedlock in 1868 to the same parents as the younger Oliver Pleasant Roberts born in 1879.

Although Mr. Land certainly used logic in many of his postings and discussions, I believe he greatly stretched reality in promoting the possibility Brushy was Billy the Kid. It appears he became seemingly convinced Brushy was Billy the Kid largely due to his interpretation of facial and handwriting comparisons, in spite of both being deemed either false or inconclusive by experts. Disregarding these conclusions, Mr. Land proceeded in the creation of scenarios aligning with Brushy's purported identity assumption of dead cousin Ollie.

As of October 20, 2014, Mr. Land's website appears at http://brushybill.proboards.com. I present three excerpts from among his many postings illustrating the context of his theory:

Be very careful about believing everything written in books. The book Billy the Kid - His Real Name Was ... by Jim Johnson claims to prove Brushy was actually lying and that his real name was Oliver Pleasant Roberts born in 1879. The logic seems very sound at face value, but there is one hole in the story which is easily missed. The book traces the life of the real Oliver Pleasant Roberts from birth in 1879 up until his marriage in 1909 and divorce in 1910. It then picks up O. L. Roberts (undoubtedly Brushy) marrying in 1912 and insists O. L. Roberts and Oliver Pleasant Roberts were the same person. I point out that Oliver Pleasant never used the middle initial L nor the nickname Ollie instead of Oliver. O. L. Roberts (Brushy) on the other hand who first shows up in the documentation in 1912 always went by Ollie or O. L.

It is entirely possible and I believe probable that Martha had two brothers named Oliver. The first being Oliver L. Roberts born in 1868 and the latter being Oliver Pleasant Roberts born in 1879. Old Henry Oliver had 10 children from two marriages and several of them lived only a year or two. He was very willing to father many children and one more that never got recorded in the census wouldn't be such a huge surprise. So I theorize that Oliver L was born to a 12 or 13 year old mother out of wedlock and was cared for by relatives. His mother Sara Elizabeth Ferguson didn't see much of him.

I believe the real Oliver Pleasant Roberts disappeared from the public record right after his embarrassing divorce in 1910. Sometime between then and 1912, Brushy (Billy the Kid) returned to Texas and took on the alias of Ollie L. Roberts.

Okay, let's analyze this theory. Since Brushy, in his interviews with Morrison, didn't mention the first Oliver marriage to Anna Lee in 1909 (a troubling one ending in divorce a year later), yet mentioned three other marriages, Mr. Land believes Oliver Pleasant Roberts vanished after divorcing Anna Lee in 1910. According to this theory, Brushy assumed the identity of Oliver L. Roberts within two years after the sudden disappearance of Oliver Pleasant Roberts. This theory portrays an older Oliver L. Roberts born in 1868 as the person Brushy impersonated, not the younger Oliver P. Roberts born in 1879. Mr. Land insists Brushy used only the name Ollie or O. L. after 1912 in public documentation, not Oliver Pleasant or O. P.

Let's assume Mr. Land's theory plausible for a momentary stretch of imagination. This scenario would require Oliver Pleasant Roberts marrying in 1909 and divorcing a year later, both in Van Zandt County. He then vanishes from all public documents, coincidentally concurrent with the sudden appearance of Oliver L. Roberts (using the name Oliver) marrying Mollie Brown in 1912 in the same county. Actually, Oliver P. did not vanish from public records after 1910, as the full name Oliver Pleasant Roberts is shown on his 1917 World War I draft registration (see Appendix I). Let's just consider Mr. Land's statement that Oliver P. vanished from public records as just a minor inaccuracy; let's continue with his theory as it further unravels.

I now provide additional evidence disproving the Oliver P. Roberts disappearance portion of Mr. Land's dubious theory. O. P. Roberts appears on two different 1918 Arkansas transactions involving the purchase and sale of 80 acres of land (see Appendices L and M). The sale of the property specifically cites the sellers as O. P. Roberts and Mollie Roberts. So, in keeping with Mr. Land's theory, both Oliver P. and Oliver L. must have had wives of the same name. In addition, leaving Arkansas after the death of Mollie in 1919 and relocating back to Van Zandt County, Texas, Oliver P. Roberts shows up on the 1920 census. Therefore, Mr. Land's claim of Oliver P. Roberts vanishing from public records after 1910 is suitably proved as false. This theory bucket is now leaking and not holding water.

Let's proceed with Mr. Land's theory even though his claim Oliver P. vanished from public records after 1910 is false. For the sake of argument, consider the possibility (no matter how remote) both Oliver P. and Oliver L.

married different ladies with the name of Mollie Brown, both dying in 1919. Allowing this as possible, we encounter additional difficulties with the unrecorded 1868 birth of a person named Oliver L. Roberts.

This element of Mr. Land's conjecture requires Henry Oliver Roberts with Sara Elizabeth Ferguson having two sons, one named Oliver Pleasant Roberts in 1879 and Oliver L. Roberts born in 1868. Let's examine this.

Henry Oliver Roberts first married in 1871 to Caroline Dunn, yielding two children, Samantha Belle and Martha Vada (my great-grandmother). Henry Oliver and Caroline remained married until the time of Caroline's death in 1874. Two years later, Henry Oliver Roberts married Sara Elizabeth Ferguson, with Oliver Pleasant Roberts as the 3rd child from this marriage.

For Mr. Land's theory of an Oliver L. born in 1868 from the same parents to be possible requires a 16 year old Henry Oliver Roberts fathering an out of wedlock son with a 12 year old Sara Elizabeth Ferguson. This would be prior to Henry Oliver's first marriage to Caroline Dunn. In addition, it would necessitate an unrecorded birth with no family records (there are records of all other children). In keeping with the issue of unfounded documental proof, no records have been located of an Oliver L. Roberts or O. L. Roberts prior to Brushy's use of the middle initial L in his 1945 marriage to Malinda Allison.

I believe I have now sufficiently shot down Mr. Land's theory. If his theory had been correct (it isn't, of course), what would it have accomplished? Mr. Land's scenario would aid the believability of only a small portion of Brushy's story. Remember, Brushy claimed assuming the identity of his dead cousin Ollie, killed in a horse theft incident in 1892. If cousin Ollie was born in 1879, he would have been only thirteen years of age at his time of death. Yet, with Mr. Land's theory of an 1868 birth year, this cousin Ollie would have been about twenty-four. In keeping with Brushy's proclaimed birth date of December 31, 1859, this would still require cousin Ollie's parents believing a thirty-three year old man was their twenty-four year old son. In addition, it would also entail Ollie's parents and half sister (Martha Vada Roberts Heath) bamboozled by Brushy's false identity for the remainder of their lives. I believe this an insurmountable stretch, don't you?

Although Brushy's name variation usage appears to be of significance to Mr. Land, I see little merit regarding Brushy's indiscriminate use of Ollie, Oliver, O. P., or Oliver Pleasant on documents throughout his life. I do note, however, the use of the middle initial *L* in marriage to his 4th wife, Malinda Allison was a departure. As discussed in an earlier chapter, I believe it likely he began using the *L* middle initial along with his fabricated birth year of 1868 as an attempt to falsely qualify for benefits as provided by the new social security law instituted in Texas in 1936.

Based on Brushy's chronological story progression, he assumed the identity of cousin Ollie in about 1892. Although it is clear the only Ollie possible from this family was Oliver Pleasant Roberts born in August of 1879, it does not appear clear to Mr. Land. At one time, Brushy indeed claimed a date of birth of December 31, 1868. During the Morrison interviews, Brushy kept the month and day the same, yet changed his birth year to 1859 becoming age appropriate for his Billy the Kid fantasy. To accommodate Brushy's tale, Mr. Land's theory would also require the non-existent older Ollie (Oliver L.) having the same month and day of birth as Brushy alleged, although with a year of 1859. The odds of that occurring are approximately 1 out of 365. Brushy's widowed wife, Malinda, did indeed apply the December 31, 1868 date on his death certificate. However, even though Malinda knew he was claiming 1859 as his birth year, I suspect she remained consistent with Brushy's previously reported 1868 birth year to avoid social security survivor benefit scrutiny.

I sincerely hope you agree Mr. Land's theory defies reasonable logic. Brushy did not assume the identity of any dead cousin Ollie. He *was* Ollie (Oliver Pleasant Roberts) and most certainly was not, Billy the Kid. As I have stated and restated many times with supported evidence throughout the pages of my book, Brushy was Oliver Pleasant Roberts born August 26, 1879. Oliver Pleasant Roberts, aka Brushy Bill Roberts, was just shy of two years of age on that historical moonlit night in 1881 when Billy the Kid was allegedly killed by Pat Garrett.

Outside photograph of fake Billy the Kid Museum in Hico, Texas.
This so-called museum promotes Brushy Bill as Billy the Kid.
Photograph provided by author's cousin, Dave Emerson.)

In Conclusion

The intent of my book was entirely for purposes of debunking the claim Brushy Bill Roberts was Billy the Kid. I have offered the reader substantial genealogical evidence and inconceivable conflicts within Brushy's own fable. The conflicts include both timeline departures from historical accounts, in addition to time and location clashes within Brushy's narrative itself. I have also provided the reader with family statements confirming Brushy's true identity as Oliver Pleasant Roberts, the name he used in one form or another throughout his life. He was born August 26, 1879 in Bates, Arkansas as the third child of Henry Oliver Roberts and Sara Elizabeth Ferguson Roberts. Oliver, aka Brushy Bill, was just shy of two years of age on the night of July 14, 1881 when Pat Garrett allegedly killed Billy the Kid. Hopefully by now, most objective readers have arrived at the conclusion Brushy (Oliver Pleasant Roberts) was not Billy the Kid.

My maternal half great-granduncle, Brushy, was simply a clever storyteller who wove an incredible yarn capturing the imagination of many. With a quick read of his imaginative fable, it appears reasonable upon first examination. However, after comparison to historical records, revelation of his actual family genealogy, and analysis of many time conflicts, the fallacy of his fable becomes apparent. His hogwash was later enhanced by clever authors creating and repeating fictional genealogy providing a better fit with Brushy's epic concoction. Over time, these falsehoods fooled many individuals (including my own mother) resulting in the Brushy believer phenomenon. After all, what could spur the imagination more than the legendary Billy the Kid escaping his final demise on a moonlit night in 1881, living on to a ripe old age. Could this be true? Maybe it is, I don't know. I leave this issue to researchers and historians. What I do know is the individual known as Brushy Bill Roberts who died from a massive heart attack on the streets of Hico, Texas was Oliver Pleasant Roberts and certainly not Billy the Kid.

In the appendices that follow, I have provided documentation referred to in the preceding text, in addition to other items of interest. One appendix item titled "Chronological Timeline for Brushy and His Locations" outlines the dates and variations of the name Oliver Pleasant Roberts used throughout his lifetime. This summary also includes recordings of his marriages and one divorce. Three of his marriages were recounted by Brushy in his interviews with Mr. Morrison. A summary of Brushy's authentic genealogy, supplementing the Roberts family tree chart shown earlier in this book, may be found in the appendices, as well.

A Short Comment from Roy Haws

I sincerely hope you have enjoyed my book. I realize comprehension of the content has been difficult due to the many names, events, and dates necessary to digest. Further complicating matters was the imaginative weaving of fact with fiction by Brushy, compounded by Brushy believer authors. If fascinated by this topic, perhaps my book will be worthy enough for a second reading. My ultimate desire is that for once and for all, we can put to rest the preposterous notion Brushy Bill Roberts was the notorious Billy the Kid. Hopefully, we all can now take Brushy's narrative for what it actually is, a whimsical and colorful fantasy.

Thank you for reading my book.

Appendix A

Certificate of Death for Ollie L. Roberts (Brushy).

TEXAS DEPARTMENT OF HEALTH
BUREAU OF VITAL STATISTICS
STATE OF TEXAS   CERTIFICATE OF DEATH   STATE FILE NO. 58415

1. PLACE OF DEATH			2. USUAL RESIDENCE (Where deceased lived. If institution: residence before admission)		
a. COUNTY Hamilton			a. STATE Texas	b. COUNTY Hamilton	
b. CITY (If outside corporate limits, write RURAL and give precinct no.) OR TOWN Hico	c. LENGTH OF STAY (In this place) 2 yrs		c. CITY (If outside corporate limits, write RURAL and give precinct no.) OR TOWN Hico		
d. FULL NAME OF (If not in hospital or institution, give street address or location) HOSPITAL OR INSTITUTION W. Second Street			d. STREET ADDRESS (If rural, give location)		

3. NAME OF DECEASED (Type or Print)	a. (First) Ollie	b. (Middle) L.	c. (Last) Roberts	4. DATE OF DEATH December 27, 1950
5. SEX Male	6. COLOR OR RACE White	7. MARRIED, NEVER MARRIED, WIDOWED, DIVORCED (Specify) Retired	8. DATE OF BIRTH Dec. 31, 1868	9. AGE YEARS 81 MONTHS 11 DAYS 26 IF UNDER 24 HRS. Hours Min.

10a. USUAL OCCUPATION (Give kind of work done during most of working life, even if retired) Retired	10b. KIND OF BUSINESS OR INDUSTRY	11. BIRTHPLACE (State or foreign country) Taylor County, Texas
12. FATHER'S NAME Unknown	BIRTHPLACE Unknown	13. MOTHER'S MAIDEN NAME Unknown BIRTHPLACE Unknown
14. WAS DECEASED EVER IN U.S. ARMED FORCES? (Yes, no, or unknown) Unknown (If yes, give war or dates of service)	15. SOCIAL SECURITY NO. Unknown	16. INFORMANT'S SIGNATURE Malinda E. Roberts

MEDICAL CERTIFICATION

17. CAUSE OF DEATH Enter only one cause per line for (a), (b), and (c)	I. DISEASE OR CONDITION DIRECTLY LEADING TO DEATH* (a) Coronary Occlusion	INTERVAL BETWEEN ONSET AND DEATH
*This does not mean the mode of dying, such as heart failure, asthenia, etc. It means the disease, injury, or complication which caused death.	ANTECEDENT CAUSES Morbid conditions, if any, giving rise to the above cause (a) stating the underlying cause last. DUE TO (b) Dropped dead on Street, Dr. W. F. Hafer Hico, Texas had been treating for DUE TO (c) Hypertensive Heart Disease	
	II. OTHER SIGNIFICANT CONDITIONS Conditions contributing to the death but not related to the disease or condition causing death. per testimony to Coroner.	

18a. DATE OF OPERATION	18b. MAJOR FINDINGS OF OPERATION	19. AUTOPSY? YES ☐ NO ☒

20a. ACCIDENT SUICIDE HOMICIDE (Specify)	20b. PLACE OF INJURY (e.g., in or about home, farm, factory, street, office bldg., etc.)	20c. (CITY, TOWN, OR PRECINCT NO.) (COUNTY) (STATE)
20d. TIME OF INJURY (Month) (Day) (Year) (Hour) m.	20e. INJURY OCCURRED WHILE AT WORK ☐ NOT WHILE AT WORK ☐	20f. HOW DID INJURY OCCUR

TEXAS DEPARTMENT OF HEALTH
REC'D JAN 2 1951
BUREAU OF VITAL STATISTICS

21. I hereby certify that I attended the deceased from ____ 19__ to ____ 19__, that I last saw the deceased alive on ____, 19__, and that death occurred at 12:50 A. M. from the causes and on the date stated above.

22a. SIGNATURE Coroner	(Degree or title)	22b. ADDRESS Hico, Texas	22c. DATE SIGNED 12/29/1950
23a. BURIAL, CREMATION, REMOVAL (Specify) Burial	23b. DATE Dec. 29, 1950	23c. NAME OF CEMETERY OR CREMATORY Hamilton Cemetery	
23d. LOCATION (City, town, or county) Hamilton (State) Texas	24. FUNERAL DIRECTOR'S SIGNATURE D. Wayne Rutledge		
25a. REGISTRAR'S FILE NO. 39	25b. DATE REC'D BY LOCAL REGISTRAR Dec. 29, 1950	25c. REGISTRAR'S SIGNATURE	

135

Appendix B

Actual Genealogical Details For Brushy.

Oliver Pleasant Roberts, aka Brushy Bill Roberts, was born 26 August 1879 in Bates, Sebastian County, Arkansas. He died on 27 December 1950 in Hico, Hamilton County, Texas.

Wives of Oliver Pleasant Roberts:

1. Anna Lee. Married 11 July 1909 in Van Zandt County, Texas; divorced 10 November 1910 in Van Zandt County, Texas.
2. Mollie Brown. Married 21 August, 1912 in Van Zandt County, Texas; died 20 February, 1919 in Little River County, Arkasas.
3. Luticia Ballard. Married 26 January 1929 in Van Zandt County, Texas; died 22 June, 1944 in Van Zandt County, Texas.
4. Malinda E. Allison. Married 13 January, 1945 in Hamilton County, Texas; died 1952 in Temple, Bell County, Texas.

Parents of Oliver Pleasant Roberts were:

Father: Henry Oliver Roberts was born in 18 May 1852 in Rusk County, Texas. He died 31 March 1924 in Van Zandt County, Texas and was buried at Hillcrest Cemetery, Van Zandt County, Texas.
Mother: Sara Elizabeth Ferguson, daughter of John W. Ferguson (b. 1830) and Martha Bolinger (b. 1837), was born 24 August 1856. She died 29 August 1924 in Van Zandt County, Texas and was buried at Hillcrest Cemetery, Van Zandt County, Texas.
Henry Oliver Roberts and Sara Elizabeth Ferguson married 14 May 1876 in Arkansas. This was the second marriage of Henry Oliver Roberts. His first marriage was to Caroline Dunn about 1871 in Arkansas. Caroline was born in October 1850 in Prairie, Franklin County, Arkansas. She died about 1874 in Arkansas.

Siblings of Oliver Pleasant Roberts were:

1. Andrew Berry Roberts was born 9 February 1877
2. Mary C. Roberts was born 17 April 1878 in Bates, Sebastian County, Arkansas; died 19 December 1968
3. John W. Roberts was born 27 June 1881 in Bates, Sebastian County, Arkansas. He died 11 September 1882 in Bates, Sebastian County, Arkansas and buried in Mount Harmony Cemetery, Greenwood, Sebastian County, Arkansas.
4. Lonnie V. Roberts was born 6 June 1884 in Sebastian County, Arkansas. He died on 30 September 1887 in Hopkins County, Texas. He was buried in Miller Grove Cemetery, Hopkins County, Texas.
5. Thomas U. Roberts was born 3 October 1885. He died in 1958.
6. Nora Roberts was born 29 April 1892 in Hopkins County, Texas. She died 6 May 1893 in Hopkins County, Texas and buried in Miller Grove Cemetery, Hopkins County, Texas.
7. Joseph Irvin Roberts was born 26 February, 1895.

Half Siblings of Oliver Pleasant Roberts (from Henry Oliver Roberts' first marriage to Caroline Dunn):

1. Samantha Belle Roberts was born 24 October 1871.
2. Martha Vada Roberts was born 3 September 1872 and died 11 December, 1947. She married Dudley Heath 6 May 1890 in Emory, Rains County, Texas. Dudley Heath was born 12 February, 1869 and died 10 December 1936.

One daughter from the marriage of Martha Vada Roberts to Dudley Heath was Vada Bell Heath. The daughter from Vada Bell's marriage to D. L. Goff was Eulaine Faye Golf. Eulaine married Leonard Haws producing three sons; the youngest, Roy Haws, is the author of this book. Vada Bell's second marriage was to Joseph Emerson. The son from that marriage is Paul Emerson.

Grandparents of Oliver Pleasant Roberts, aka Brushy Bill Roberts, were:

Grandfather: Joseph Roberts was born 1797 in Virginia. He died 22 February 1857 in Rusk County, Texas.
Grandmother: Rachel Henson was the daughter of James Baret Henson and Elizabeth Ann Talley. Rachel was born 11 September 1828 in Rabun or Gilmer County, Georgia.

Joseph and Rachel (Oliver's grandparents) were married 28 July 1844 in Rusk County, Texas.

Siblings of Oliver's father, Henry Oliver Roberts, were:

1. Virgil A. Roberts was born 2 March 1847 and died 1 March 1928.
2. Amanda Roberts was born 29 July 1849 and died 12 January 1923.
3. Samantha E. Roberts was born June 1850.
4. Andrew B. Roberts was born 17 October 1854 and died 24 August 1910.

Appendix C

Chronological Timeline For Brushy (Oliver Pleasant Roberts)
and His Locations (from public records).

August 26, 1879 (Oliver Pleasant Roberts). Birth in Bates, Sebastian County, Arkansas

June 1, 1880 Census (Oliver Roberts, Age 1). Bates, Sebastian County, Arkansas

June 5, 1900 Census (Oliver P., Age 20). Sulphur Springs, Hopkins County, Texas

July 11, 1909 (O. P. Roberts). Marriage to Anna Lee, Van Zandt County, Texas

May 2, 1910 Census. (Oliver P. Roberts, Age 30), Van Zandt County, Texas

September 17, 1910 (O. P. Roberts). Filed for Divorce from Anna Lee, Van Zandt County, Texas

November 10, 1910 (O. P. Roberts). Divorce of Anna Lee, Van Zandt County, Texas

August 21, 1912 (Oliver Roberts). Marriage to Mollie Brown, Van Zandt County, Texas

February 26, 1918 (O. P. Roberts). Warranty Deed, Purchase of 80 acres of land, Sevier County, Arkansas

August 21, 1918 (O. P. Roberts). Warranty Deed, Sale of 80 acres of land, Sevier County, Arkansas

September 12, 1918 (Oliver Pleasant Roberts). Draft Registration, Arkinda, Little River County, Arkansas

February 20, 1919 (Ollie Roberts). Death of Mollie Brown Roberts, Little River County, Arkansas

January 9, 1920 Census (Oliver P. Roberts, age 41). Van Zandt County, Texas

January 26, 1929 (O. Roberts). Marriage to Luticia Ballard, Van Zandt County, Texas

April 17, 1930 Census (Oliver Roberts, Age 52). Van Zandt County, Texas

April 1, 1940 Census (Ollie Roberts, Age 70). Gladewater, Gregg County, Texas

June 22, 1944 (Ollie Roberts). Death Certificate for Luticia Ballard Roberts, Van Zandt County, Texas

January 14, 1945 (O. L. Roberts). Marriage to Malinda E. Allison, Hamilton County, Texas

June 1949 Brushy began his interviews with William V. Morrison

August 1949 (O. L. Roberts). Moved from Hamilton, Texas to Hico, Texas. Both in Hamilton County, Texas

September 6, 1949 (O. L. Roberts). Taped interview with Morrey Davidson as a witness asserting J. Frank Dalton was the historical Jesse James (not a public record, but taped interview in possession of author)

November 29, 1950 (O. L. Roberts). Brushy's public Interview with New Mexico Governor Mabry

December 27, 1950 (Ollie L. Roberts). His death certificate, Hico, Hamilton County, Texas

Appendix D

Chronological Summary of Brushy's Many Falsehoods. This is a detailed summary of
Brushy's falsehoods, other than those during the Lincoln County War era.
His false statements regarding the period of time from 1878–1881 are
considerably discussed in the text of my book.

1832. March 8. Date Brushy claimed as the date of birth of his father, James Henry
Roberts near Lexington, Kentucky.
Note: This James Henry Roberts did not exist. Brushy's father was Henry Oliver
Roberts born May, 1852 in Texas.

1835. Year Brushy claimed his grandfather, Ben settled in Nacogdoches, Texas.
Note: Brushy's grandfather was Joseph Roberts born in 1797 in Virginia and
eventually settled in Rusk County, Texas in the 1840s.

1859. December 31. Brushy claimed as his date of birth in Buffalo Gap, Texas with
the name William Henry Roberts.
Note: Brushy was actually born August 26, 1879 as Oliver Pleasant Roberts in Bates,
Arkansas.

1862. Year Brushy claimed his mother, Mary Adeline Dunn Roberts died.
Note: Mary Adeline Dunn Roberts married to a James Henry (or J. H.) Roberts never
existed. It would be 17 more years before Brushy (Oliver Pleasant Roberts)
would be born.

1867. Year Brushy told Morrison in his interview when "Ollie" Roberts was born.
This is the identity Brushy claimed to impersonate through most of his mature
life, although he later used the birth date of December 31, 1868 on documents.
Brushy's widowed wife also used December 31, 1868 on his original tombstone.
Note: In the Morrison interviews, Brushy claimed his birth date was December 31,
1859. There was no "Ollie" Roberts born to the Henry Oliver Roberts family for
either 1867 or 1868. The only "Ollie" in this family was Oliver Pleasant Roberts

born August 26, 1879. Brushy even used the full name of Oliver Pleasant Roberts on his draft registration in 1917. There was no impersonation. Brushy was Oliver Pleasant Roberts.

1869. Brushy claimed his "mother" treated a wound of Jesse James.
Note: At this time, consistent with Brushy's story, he would have been under the care of his claimed half aunt Catherine Bonney McCarty. Brushy's named locations of Catherine do not appear to coincide with those of Jesse James at this time. With Brushy's account, he would have been ten (or seven) years of age, but it would be another ten years before Brushy (Oliver Pleasant Roberts) would be born in Arkansas.

1872. Year Brushy claimed leaving his half aunt, Catherine Bonney McCarty Antrim in Silver City, New Mexico returning to his father, James Henry Roberts in Carlton, Texas.
Note: From historical accounts, Catherine McCarty Antrim did not arrive in Silver City, New Mexico until 1873. Henry McCarty, aka Billy the Kid, was in Silver City, New Mexico until September 1875. Catherine McCarty Antrim was Henry's mother, not his half aunt. James Henry Roberts in Carlton, Texas never existed and James Henry was not Brushy's father. It would be 7 more years before Brushy (Oliver Pleasant Roberts) would be born in Arkansas.

1874. May. Year and month Brushy claimed escaping from his father (James Henry Roberts), joining a cattle drive leading to the Indian Territory, and experiencing escapades including employment by Belle Reed (later known as Belle Starr).
Note: Henry McCarty, aka Billy the Kid, was still in Silver City, New Mexico. Belle Reed resided in Texas at this time. James Henry Roberts was not Brushy's father and did not exist. It would be more than 5 years before Brushy (Oliver Pleasant Roberts) would be born.

1874. September. Brushy claimed returning to Silver City, NM when his half aunt Catherine died.
Note: Shortly after the funeral, Brushy claimed departing with his friend Mountain Bill on an escapade lasting several years. Billy the Kid, however, remained in Silver City, New Mexicp until an escape from jail after a theft incident in September 1875.

1876. June 23-26. Historical date of Custer's battle with Indians culminating in the Battle of Little Big Horn. Brushy stated Kit Carson and his father, James Henry

Roberts, told Custer they could not defeat the five tribes, but Custer would not listen to them.

Note: Kit Carson died May 23, 1868, more than eight years before the battle. In addition, James Henry Roberts was not Brushy's father and never existed. It would be 3 more years before Brushy (Oliver Pleasant Roberts) would be born.

1877-1881. Brushy claimed a number of experiences during this period of time shortly before, during, and after the Lincoln County War culminating with his alleged death at the hands of Pat Garrett July 14, 1881.

Note: In the preceding text, I have a revealed a number of Brushy's false statements regarding this period. For this item, I will only summarize by stating Brushy (Oliver Pleasant Roberts) was certainly not in Lincoln County, New Mexico and either not yet born or under two years of age during this period.

1884. The year Brushy claimed his cousin "Ollie" ran away from home. Brushy asserted assuming the identity of his dead cousin in about 1892.

Note: Brushy did not assume the identity of dead cousin Ollie because Brushy was "Ollie" (Oliver Pleasant Roberts).

1888-1893. Brushy named a large number of employments and experiences during this period.

Note: It was impossible to have accomplished all stated employments in the given time (see the discussion and detail in item # 9 in my chapter titled "Other Holes in Brushy's Story"). During this range of time, Brushy (Oliver Pleasant Roberts) would have been 9 to 14 years of age.

1889-1914. Approximate timeframe when Brushy claimed to have operated his own Wild West show (he claimed 25 years).

Note: Many problems with this claim including overlapping employments, timeline difficulties, and no record found of any such show.

1892. Approximate year Brushy claimed finding dead cousin "Ollie" and returning his belongings to the family in Sulphur Springs, Texas. "Ollie's" mother (Sara Elizabeth Ferguson Roberts) accepted him as her long lost son. He reported seeing his cousin Martha and her husband Dudley Heath.

Note: Sara Elizabeth Ferguson Roberts was Brushy's birth mother. Brushy was "Ollie". Martha was his half sister, not cousin. In 1892, "Ollie" (Brushy) would have been only 13 years of age.

1892. June. Brushy claimed while employed as a deputy marshal for the U.S. Marshal Service, he failed in his attempt to stop a Dalton Gang train robbery resulting in the death of a Deputy.
Note: Historical accounts do not indicate a Dalton Gang train heist in June 1892 nor records of a Deputy U.S. Marshall killed.

1894. Fall. Brushy claimed to have rejoined the U.S. Marshal force serving three more years.
Note: Conflicts with Brushy's claim of simultaneously ranching in Mexico through 1896 and 1897.

1898. Spring. Brushy claimed enlisting as one Roosevelt's Rough Riders and fighting in the Spanish American War.
Note: I have discussed this false claim in my chapter "Brushy' Timeline Conflicts" in my item #12. Brushy's was not part of this expedition and his account departs significantly from historical facts.

1899. June . Brushy described thirty-six cowboys (including himself) battling two thousand Mexican soldiers in Mexico.
Note: In 1899, Brushy was still living in his parents' home in Sulphur Springs, Texas.

1907. Brushy claimed establishing a ranch known as Three Bar Ranch in Mexico, participating in the Mexican revolution in 1910, and not leaving Mexico until 1914.
Note: Brushy married in 1909, divorced in 1910, and married again in 1912 all in Van Zandt County, Texas. With his second wife Mollie Brown, Brushy described many employments from 1912-1919, none of which were in Mexico.

1912-1919. Brushy described a number of his employments from the time of his marriage to Mollie Brown through the year of her death.
Note: Brushy had earlier claimed to have been in Mexico from 1907-1914. Brushy described competing in bucking horse events while his claimed age would have been 53, a bit old for such events. Brushy related working as an officer during the oil boom in East Texas. The oil boom didn't begin until 1930.

1949. Brushy stated he never told anyone he was Billy the Kid until the time of his interviews with Morrison in 1949.
Note: It is clear Brushy had been making this claim for a number of years including family, friends, and on the streets of Hamilton and Hico, Texas where he would trap people to tell his yarn to anyone who would listen.

1950 - November. During testimony with Governor Mabry, Brushy contended he did not kill anyone during his escape from the Lincoln County Courthouse in April 1881. He claimed to have just escaped and rode his horse out of Lincoln.

Note: History is clear Billy the Kid killed Deputies Olinger and Bell during his escape. I should also note that during questioning, Brushy could not even remember Pat Garrett's name. Brushy was without the aid of his notebooks used during the earlier interviews with Mr. Morrison.

Appendix E

Marriage Certificate for O. P. Roberts and Anna Lee.

47. Appendix F

Decree of Divorce for O. P. Roberts and Anna Lee.

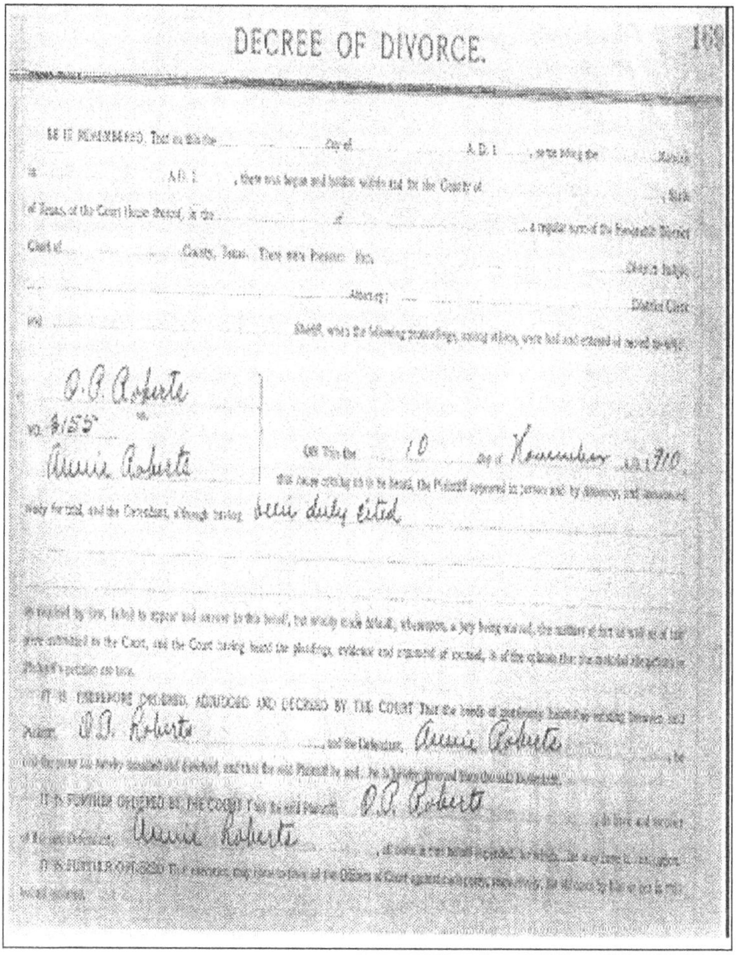

DECREE OF DIVORCE. 169

O. P. Roberts
vs.
No. 1155
Annie Roberts

On This the 10 day of November A.D. 1910

been duly cited

IT IS THEREFORE ORDERED, ADJUDGED AND DECREED BY THE COURT

Plaintiff, O. P. Roberts, and the Defendant, Annie Roberts

IT IS FURTHER ORDERED BY THE COURT that the said Plaintiff, O. P. Roberts

of the said Defendant, Annie Roberts

Appendix G

Marriage Certificate for Oliver Roberts and Mollie Brown.

Appendix H

Marriage License for Oliver Roberts and Mollie Brown.

Appendix I

Draft Registration for Oliver Pleasant Roberts.

Appendix J

Certificate of Death for Luticia Roberts.

APPENDIX K

Marriage Record for O. L. Roberts
to Malinda E. Allison.

Appendix L

O. P. Roberts

Purchase of 80 acres of Arkansas Land for $500 in February 1918.

WARRANTY DEED
WITH RELINQUISHMENT OF DOWER

KNOW ALL MEN BY THESE PRESENTS: That we, *J. M. Moses*
and *Laura Moses* his wife,
for and in consideration of the sum of ($500.00) *Five Hundred* Dollars,
and other valuable considerations, the receipt of which is hereby acknowledged in full payment,

do hereby Grant, Bargain, Sell and Convey unto the said *O. P. Roberts*
and unto *his* heirs and assigns, forever, the following lands
lying in the County of *Sevier* and State of Arkansas, to-wit:

The (NE¼ of NE¼) Northeast Quarter of the Northeast Quarter of Section (28) Twenty-eight and the (NW¼ of the NW¼) Northwest Quarter of the Northwest Quarter of Section (27) Twenty-seven, Township (7) Seven, South Range (31) Thirty-one West, containing (80) Eighty acres.

(20 ¢ Revenue Stamp attached)

TO HAVE AND TO HOLD THE SAME Unto the said *O. P. Roberts*
and unto *his* heirs and assigns forever, with all appurtenances thereunto belonging. And *we* hereby covenant with
said *O. P. Roberts*
that *we* will forever Warrant and Defend the title to the said lands against all claims whatever.

And I, *Laura Moses* wife of the said *J. M. Moses*
for and in consideration of the said sum of money, do hereby release and relinquish unto the said *O. P. Roberts*
all of my right of dower and homestead in and to the said lands.

WITNESS our hands and seals, this *25th* day of *Feb*, 191*8*.

J. M. Moses [L. S.]

Laura Moses [L. S.]

O. P. Roberts & Mollie Roberts.
Sale of Same 80 acres of Arkansas Land for $800 in August 1918.

WARRANTY DEED
WITH RELINQUISHMENT OF DOWER.

KNOW ALL MEN BY THESE PRESENTS: That we, *O. P. Roberts* his wife,

and *Mollie Roberts*

for and in consideration of the sum of *($800.00) Eight Hundred no/100* Dollars,

Paid , E. B. Green the receipt of which is hereby acknowledged in full payment

do hereby Grant, Bargain, Sell and Convey unto the said *E. B. Green*

and unto *his* heirs and assigns, forever, the following lands,

lying in the County of *Sevier* and State of Arkansas, to-wit;

The N. E¼ of the N. E¼ Sec. 28 and N. W¼ of the N. W¼ Sec. 27 all in Tp. 7 S. R. 31 West, containing 80 acres more or less.

($1.00 Revenue Stamp Attached)

TO HAVE AND TO HOLD THE SAME Unto the said *E. B. Green*

and unto *his* heirs and assigns forever, with all appurtenances thereunto belonging. And *we* hereby covenant with

said *E. B. Green*

that *we* will forever Warrant and Defend the title to the said lands against all claims whatever.

And I, *Mollie Roberts* wife of the said *O. P. Roberts*

for and in consideration of the said sum of money, do hereby release and relinquish unto the said

E. B. Green

all of my right of dower and homestead in and to the said lands.

WITNESS our hands and seals, this *21* day of *August*, 191*8*.

O. P. Roberts [L. S.]

Mollie Roberts [L. S.]

ACKNOWLEDGMENT

STATE OF ARKANSAS, } ss.

County of *Sevier*

BE IT REMEMBERED, That on this day, came before me, the undersigned, *Notary Public* within and for the County aforesaid, duly commissioned and acting *O. P. Roberts* to me well known as the Grantor in the foregoing Deed, and stated that *he* has executed the same for the consideration and purpose therein mentioned and set forth.

And on the same day also voluntarily appeared before me, *the said Mollie Roberts* wife said *O. P. Roberts* to me well known, and in the absence of her said husband declared that she had of her own free will, executed said Deed and signed and sealed the relinquishment of dower and homestead in the said Deed for the consideration and purposes therein contained and set forth, without compulsion or undue influence of her husband.

WITNESS my hand and seal as such *Notary Public* on this *21* day of *Aug* 191*8*

My Commission expires *Mch 17, 1921*

D. M. Kennedy

N. P.

Filed for record on this *31st* day of *August* A. D. 191*8*, at *3* o'clock, *A* M.

Tom Edwards

Clerk and Ex-Officio Recorder.

By _____ D.

Appendix N

Certificate of Death for Martha Vada Roberts Heath (Brushy's half sister) showing father as H. O. Roberts and mother's maiden name as Dunn.

1. PLACE OF DEATH STATE OF TEXAS	TEXAS DEPARTMENT OF HEALTH
COUNTY OF Cherokee	BUREAU OF VITAL STATISTICS
CITY OR PRECINCT NO. Jacksonville	STANDARD CERTIFICATE OF DEATH

2. FULL NAME OF DECEASED Martha Vada Heath ... 619 Edwards
Give Street and Number or name of Institution

LENGTH OF RESIDENCE WHERE DEATH OCCURRED 25 YEARS ... MONTHS ... DAYS (SOCIAL SECURITY NO.)
RESIDENCE OF THE DECEASED Street and No. 619 Edwards City Jacksonville County Cherokee State Texas

PERSONAL AND STATISTICAL PARTICULARS

3. SEX Female

4. COLOR OR RACE White

5. SINGLE, MARRIED, WIDOWED OR DIVORCED (Write the Word) Widowed

6. DATE OF BIRTH Sept. 3, 1873

7. AGE Years 74 Months 3 Days 8 IF LESS than 1 day ... Hours ... Min.

8A. TRADE, PROFESSION OR KIND OF WORK DONE housewife
8B. INDUSTRY OR BUSINESS IN WHICH ENGAGED

9. BIRTHPLACE (State or Country) Ark

10. NAME H. O. Roberts
11. BIRTHPLACE (State or Country) Unknown
12. MAIDEN NAME Dunn
13. BIRTHPLACE (State or Country) Unknown
14. SIGNATURE A. B. Heath

ADDRESS Ft. Worth TEXAS

15. PLACE OF BURIAL OR REMOVAL Old Palestine TEXAS
DATE Dec. 13, 1947

16. Gregory-Spraggins by H. L. Swofford

ADDRESS Jacksonville TEXAS

MEDICAL PARTICULARS

17. DATE OF DEATH Dec. 11, 1947

18. I HEREBY CERTIFY that I attended the deceased from July ... 194 6 to Dec. 11 194 7
I last saw her alive on Dec. 10 194 7
the death occurred on the date stated above at 4:50 P M
THE PRIMARY CAUSE OF DEATH WAS: DURATION

Coronary Thrombosis

CONTRIBUTORY CAUSES WERE
Myocardial infarction
Arteriosclerosis

If not due to disease, specify whether:
ACCIDENT, SUICIDE, OR HOMICIDE
DATE OF OCCURRENCE
PLACE OF OCCURRENCE
MANNER OR MEANS
IF RELATED TO OCCUPATION OF DECEASED, SPECIFY

SIGNATURE Geo M. Hillard M D
ADDRESS Jacksonville TEXAS

20. FILE NUMBER 12-12-47 194 SIGNATURE OF LOCAL REGISTRAR R. J. Underhill POSTOFFICE ADDRESS Jacksonville TEXAS
FILE DATE

IF DECEASED HAS RENDERED MILITARY SERVICE, FILL OUT THE FOLLOWING:
(1) Is the deceased reported to have been in such service?
(3) Serial number of discharge papers or adjusted service certificate?
Post Office Address
(2) Name of organization in which service was rendered?
(4) Name of next of kin or of next friend?

PLEASE FILL IN FOR ALL DEATHS

Name of husband or wife
What operation was performed?
Was autopsy performed?
Age in years
For what disease or condition?
What were the findings?

RECORDED this 6th day of December 19 48

STATE OF TEXAS

County of Cherokee

I HEREBY CERTIFY that the above certificate is a true and accurate copy of the record of death of

Martha Vada Heath

filed in my office, and is of record on

Page 600 Vol 14 of the Records of Deaths of Cherokee County, Texas.

Witness my hand and seal of office this 31st day of January 19 89

Fairy Upshaw

By _Deborah Miller_ Deputy. County Clerk Cherokee County, Texas.

Bibliography

BOOKS/PUBLICATIONS REFERENCED IN CONTENT:

Burns, Walter Noble. *The Saga of Billy the Kid*, University of New Mexico Press, 1999.

Cooper, Gale. *Billy the Kid's Pretenders*, Gelcour Books, 2010.

Cunningham, Eugene. *Triggernometry*, Caxton Printers, 1941.

Fleming, Elvis E. *Treasures of History IV - Historical Events of Chaves County, New Mexico*, iUniverse, Inc., 2003.

Garrett, Pat F. *The Authentic Life of Billy the Kid*, Indian Head Books, 1994. New Edition, Sunstone Press, 2007.

Jameson, W. C. *The Return of the Outlaw Billy the Kid*, Republic of Texas Press, 1998.

——— *Billy the Kid Beyond the Grave*, Taylor Trade Publishing, 2005.

——— *Billy the Kid The Lost Interviews*, Garlic Press Publishing, 2012.

Johnson, Jim. *Billy the Kid, His Real Name Was...*, Outskirts Press, 2006.

Lemay, John and Burnett, Roger K. *Legendary Locals of Roswell*, Arcadia Publishing, Charleston, SC, 2012.

Nolan, Frederick. *The West of Billy the Kid*, University of Oklahoma Press, 1998.

Sonnichsen, C. L. and Morrison, William V. *Alias Billy the Kid*, University of New Mexico Press, 1955.

Tunstill, William A. *Billy the Kid and Me Were the Same*, Western History Research Center, 1988.

Turner, Thomas. Newspaper article dated September 18, 1950 titled *"Texan Knew Bad Men, Saw Hoss Thieves Hang"* from *Dallas Morning News*.

Unknown. *A Memorial and Biographical History of Hill County, Texas*, 1892.

OTHER BOOK SOURCE INFORMATION:

Bell, Bob Boze. *The Illustrated Life and Times of Billy the Kid*, Tri Star Boze Publications, 2004

Cline, Donald. *Alias Billy the Kid, The Man Behind the Legend*, Sunstone Press, 1986.

Hall, Brett L. *The Real Billy the Kid AKA Brushy Bill Roberts*, LuLu Press, 2011.

Hefner, Bobby E. *The Trial of Billy the Kid,* Bosque River Publishing, 1991.

Jacobsen, Joel. *Such Men as Billy the Kid,* University of Nebraska Press, 1994.

Kadlec, Robert F. *They Knew Billy the Kid,* Ancient City Press, 1987.

Miller, Jay. *Billy the Kid Rides Again, Digging for the Truth,* Sunstone Press, 2005.

Otero, Miguel Antonio Jr. *The Real Billy the Kid,* Arte Publico Press, Houston, Texas, 1998.

Poe, John William. *The Death of Billy the Kid,* Facsimile of Original 1933 Edition, Sunstone Press, 2006.

Simmons, Marc .*When Six-Guns Ruled,* Ancient City Press, Santa Fe, New Mexico, 1990.

Siringo, Charles A. *History of Billy the Kid,* Chas. A. Siringo, 1920

Utley, Robert M. *Billy the Kid, A Short and Violent Life,* University of Nebraska Press, 1989.

Valdez, Dr. Jannay P. and Hefner. Judge Bobby *Billy the Kid: Killed in New Mexico Died in Texas,* Outlaw Publications, 1994.

WEBSITE AND OTHER SOURCES

Billy the Kid Outlaw Gang, Taiban, New Mexico, accessed October 20, 2014, (www.billythekidoutlawgang.com/)

Daughters of the Republic on Ancestry.com, Roberts Family, accessed October 20, 2014, (*www.rootsweb.ancestry.com/~txccmdrt/roberts_benjamin.htm*)

Davidson, Morrey, *The True Jesse James Story*, taped interview of September 6, 1949. The interview was during a birthday celebration for J. Frank Dalton who claimed to be Jesse James. One of the witnesses was Brushy, identified as O. L. Roberts.

Heritage Auctions *William Uncle Kit Carson.* Historical.ha.com.. accessed Oct 20, 2014

Land, Wayne *Brushy's Handwriting - Brushy Bill Billy the Kid Message Board, Proboards.Web, accessed October 20, 2014*

Weathers, Elreeta *Brushy Bill or Billy the Kid?, Gazetter of Hamilton County, Texas, 2000, Roots Web, 1 Jan 2006, accessed October 20, 2014*

INDEX

www.ingramcontent.com/pod-product-compliance
Lightning Source LLC
Chambersburg PA
CBHW021403090426
42742CB00009B/990